Ladies of Letters

Ladies of Letters

IRENE SPENCER AND VERA SMALL

(LOU WAKEFIELD)   (CAROLE HAYMAN)

Futura

A Futura Book

First published in Great Britain in 1991 by
Futura Publications,
a Division of Macdonald & Co (Publishers) Ltd,
London & Sydney

ISBN 0 7088 4531 2

Typeset by Leaper & Gard Ltd, Bristol, England
Printed and bound in Great Britain by
BPCC Hazell Books
Aylesbury, Bucks, England
Member of BPCC Ltd.

Futura Publications
A Division of
Macdonald & Co (Publishers) Ltd
165 Great Dover Street
London SE1 4YA

A member of Maxwell Macmillan Publishing Corporation

Foreword

Casa Richa
Marbella
Espanol

Ladies of Letters

Knowing my interest in collecting historical documents my friends Lou Wakefield and Carole Hayman passed me a bundle of letters after finding them in the drawer of a melamine bedside cabinet (which was being offered for sale at a car boot sale in Walmer, Kent). The correspondence is between a Mrs Spencer and a Mrs Small.

I have spent many a night with those important letters spread out in front of me. How homesick I felt for England.

What fascinating glimpses of lower middle-class life they afford. How Irene Spencer and Vera Small suffered for their families. Medals should be struck in their honour.

Irene is a 'plain cook' and Vera an 'exotic', which says it all perhaps. But, despite these differences, a friendship grows and a relationship develops. These unknown women (sadly neither are now to be found at the same addresses, and the Salvation Army has drawn a blank), these bastions of English society have unknowingly presented us with an accurate social document. Clippings from the local press provide welcome background material. Thanks to Vera and Irene future generations will be able to read this book and know what it was like to live in the late nineteen eighties.

Social historians wishing to know what a 'knitted thermal boob tube' is will turn to this book in gratitude.

The letters are indeed fascinating on matters domestic (the book is awash with household hints and recipes), but broad social issues are not neglected. Irene writes to Vera from Grossthorpe police cells after her arrest for contravening the Public Order Act and events take a dramatic turn when both ladies are subsequently imprisoned aboard H.M. Prison Ship *Pride of Cleveland*. But typically, they manage to maintain their correspondence by the ingenious use of prison issue toilet paper. Others are drawn into the correspondence. Vera's son Howard, a somewhat regressive type, writes to his mother on organic brown rice paper informing her that he is suffering from alopecia. Karen, Vera's daughter, is in permanent crisis, and Bruce, a Church of England clergyman, writes from the vicarage on both sides of a communion wafer. But it is Irene, released on the grounds of insanity, who battles for her friend Vera's freedom, organising a *Vera Small is Mad Appeal, Fork and Finger Buffet*.

These letters will appeal to anyone who is on a rota to arrange church flowers, those interested in penal reform, and students of family life. I found them to be quite compelling. Quite honestly as I laid the last letter aside I felt a better person for having glimpsed behind the net curtains of Mrs Small and Mrs Spencer's turbulent lives. And to think that Ms Hayman and Ms Wakefield almost used this precious archive to line a ferret's cage. That the ferret expired before they could do so surely points to the existence of God.

Sue Townsend
Marbella 1991

34 Wormwold Way
Hethergreen

14th July

Dear Vera,

Thank you for your 'thank you' letter of the 9th – yes, it was a lovely day. I had a postcard from Lesley and Keith this morning from Lanzarote, food superb, weather glorious, gorgeous hotel – I shall pop round to the new house tomorrow to order the milk and papers.

It was kind of you to write a thank you note. So few people bother now – you'd be surprised out of a hundred guests and thirty-five others who were posted cake, how many just don't seem to think. I did enjoy your company at the reception, and am much obliged for the loan of your handkerchief (laundered and returned, enclosed). It seems a shame you live so far away, since we seem to share so many of the same interests. Perhaps we'll become pen-pals instead!

Must close as Sidney is howling for his tea. The house seems so empty now, I'm glad of his company, so he's getting a bit spoilt I'm afraid.

The secret of my taramasalata dip is that I mix the roe with cottage cheese, and perhaps a *few* breadcrumbs, so that it is not too oily. It always proves popular at parties.

Kind regards,

Irene Spencer

Gables
Little Potterton

16th July

Dear Irene,

Thank you so much for your note thanking me for my 'thank you' letter. I quite agree that not enough people bother these days. Courtesy costs nothing, I always say (unless you count 17p for the stamp! Isn't it an awful price!) I felt quite down when I returned home. I do love an 'occasion' and now my children are both so far away I don't often get them. In fact the last was Gerald's funeral. Still, I mustn't complain.

You will miss Lesley at first, I am sure. She is a lovely girl and looked quite magical in her wedding gown. Ivory taffeta has always been a favourite of mine – I was so glad when Princess Diana decided on it. Still, Keith seems a pleasant chap. I tried your taramasalata on the vicar's wife and she said she'd never tasted anything like it. Exchange is no robbery, so here is one of my standbys.

Crumble a packet of digestive biscuits into a pan of bitter-sweet melted chocolate and butter. Mix well. Turn into a flat pie dish and press well down. Pop into the freezer. Delicious as a teatime snack or cut into squares as petit fours. Gerald always had a very sweet tooth.

Well, I must close now as it is time for 'A Book at Bedtime'. It's the 'Boston Strangler' this week. Do let's keep in touch. I love to get a letter in the morning. It makes the day, I feel. Of course the children write – when they can.

All the best,

Vera

34 Wormwold Way
Hethergreen

21st July

Dear Vera,

Your letter has thrown me into utter mental turmoil and I haven't slept a wink since receiving it. I've not been able to settle to anything, and finally I thought, well, you'll just have to face her with it, so that is what I am doing. After all, honesty's the best policy, and if in doubt, say you don't know.

Now, I'm going to say some things in total confidence, and I'll hope that it will go no further. I should hate everybody to think I was a fool, even if I am. It's so very embarrassing, I don't know how to put it. Of course you know that I had a hundred guests to invite. Well, Lesley and Keith wrote out a list, and Keith's parents, and I added mine to it, so I lost track a bit of who was who. Things are such a burden when you're on your own (as of course you know) – there's so much to keep in your mind. Still, no excuses, fair's fair. The long and the short of it is, I thought you were one of Keith's family when I met you. It wasn't until in your last letter you said 'Lesley is a lovely girl ... Keith seems a pleasant chap', that I had the inkling of an idea that you weren't one of his aunties. I could have sworn that's what somebody said at the reception. Are you perhaps one of Lesley's old teachers, or a friend from where she used to work? I know she had some coming. Please don't say you are one of my family, or I think I shall go quite mad. Perhaps I am already. I do forget people's names now I'm older, and I mislay things constantly.

Proof of the pudding: I just made myself a cup of Ovaltine after that last sentence, and then I couldn't find my

3

pen. I searched high and low. Finally I found it behind my ear. I *never* put a pen behind my ear, I don't think. You see, I feel now that I can't be sure of anything any more. I've really come to mistrust myself. This is how old ladies are supposed to go isn't it? But I'm only sixty-two. I dare hardly go to the shops any more, in case I walk out and forget to pay like Lady Barnett used to: and look what happened to her!

Now, I hope this won't spoil our friendship, because I did so enjoy your company. I've certainly not danced a tango like that in years – before I was married in fact. And this brings me to my second point. I do remember that we enjoyed a quantity of liquid libation, and in the heat of the moment I might have broken the rule of a lifetime and uttered one or two confidences to you. I shan't say what they were, in case I didn't. There are a couple of small things of a personal nature that I'd rather not tell the world and his wife, if you know what I mean, and if I did tell you, then please, please, forget them.

Oh dear, all this sounds very dramatic doesn't it? I'm not usually an emotional person, I can assure you. Perhaps it's the shock of Lesley and Keith deciding to stay a week longer. I've had to go and cancel the milk and papers and turn everything off, and of course the newsagent looked at me as if I were a perfect fool. If they'd come home as planned, I could have asked Lesley who you were, but then again perhaps I wouldn't have. Children get so irritable when you forget things don't they?

Please forgive this outburst. I'm sure it's all a simple misunderstanding.

With sincerest good wishes,

Irene

P.S. I've been too depressed to make up your recipe yet, but it sounds delicious.

30th July

My dear Irene,

Sorry to have been a while answering your letter. The postman (silly fool) unfortunately delivered it to the wrong 'Gables' – the one in *Great* Potterton – and Mrs Wavertree was two days bringing it round (she finds it hard to get out with her arthritic knee). Then she delivered it when I was out and the dog hid it in her basket. I discovered it, partly chewed, when I gave her blanket a good shake this morning.

I was upset to think you have been on tenterhooks waiting for my answer. I *do* know what you mean about this absent-minded business. Only yesterday I set off to the shop for toilet paper and came back with a tin of Cherry Blossom and twenty cigarettes. I wouldn't mind, but I haven't smoked since I was twelve! Sometimes I think I would forget my own name if it wasn't on a chain round my neck. Karen gave it to me for my last birthday and I wonder if it wasn't a hint.

To put your mind at rest, no, we have never met before, and I'm not really from either 'side'. I'm an old friend of Betty's and as I was staying with her when she 'masterminded' your catering I thought I might as well give her a hand. The Salmon Mousse and the Blue Cheese Quiche were mine. Betty and I used to do 'functions' together before I moved. More a hobby than anything really.

I *do* recall having one or two sherries, but I've no memory at all of dancing the tango. Are you sure it was me? Gerald always used to say I had two left feet, though I was considered quite a jitterbugger in my youth. As to any confidences, I can assure you they are quite safe with me. Betty says I passed out as soon as I got in the car, and the next morning I left as soon as I had drunk a black coffee. I

5

would have liked to have lingered, but Mabel Thrush (my next-door neighbour) would only look after the dog until Sunday.

It's nice to think that you felt you could confide in me though, on so short an acquaintance. I've often longed for a friend to talk about 'personal' matters. Men don't encourage intimacy do they? I always felt rather a hysterical fool if I got 'emotional' about anything with Gerald. How have you filled your extra week without Lesley and Keith? Pity I didn't know sooner or you could have popped up here for a couple of days ... Must stop now as Mabel is at the door. I expect she's 'on the borrow' again. Take care of yourself and steer clear of the sherry bottle!

All the best,

Vera

2nd August

Dear Vera,

Thank you for your letter, albeit tardy. Lesley and Keith are back from Lanzarote now, and it's nice to have things back to normal. I apologise for my letter. I have been under the doctor recently but am better now thanks to the tablets.

I don't know quite what you mean by your parting remark about staying away from the sherry bottle. Tippling has never been a vice I have fallen foul of, and sherry has never been my drink. If you are gaining your impressions from the reception, I can assure you that that was the exception that proves the rule, and if a mother can't get tipsy at her only daughter's wedding, I don't know what to think.

Thank you for your offer to stay with you, albeit in retrospect, but I should have had to refuse. I can't leave Sidney on his own, and Lesley is the only one besides me that he can tolerate, and who know his habits.

I have tried your recipe, but I found it rather rich.

Yours sincerely,

Irene Spencer

7

'The Gables'

10th August

Dear Irene,

Just a note to let you know I've had a little spell in hospital since I last wrote. Sorry it's so short but I've still got my arm in a sling. The fact is that I had a silly fall the very morning your letter arrived! I was running upstairs to get my writing paper and the dog (she's forever under my feet) had parked herself right at the top. I don't know why – perhaps I was in a bit of a state – but I just didn't see her and down I went. I've had concussion, cracked ribs and a nasty sprained wrist. Hope you are keeping well.

Yours,

Vera

12th August

Dear Vera,

Words cannot express the shame and remorse I feel at having caused you such misery. Are you very poorly? Of course you are, what a stupid question! I remember only too well when I sprained my ankle on the garage door, to conjure up visions of black swelling and agony. It is one of those swing-up-and-over affairs, and Clive was in such a hurry to watch the cricket and was hooting at me to make haste. Somehow my slacks had got caught up in the mechanism, and as I threw the door upwards, I suddenly found myself hanging upside down, suspended by one leg. The pain when I came round was excruciating (the Doctor said I'd been lucky to escape a fracture), and I was too much in physical distress to see the humorous side of it, which Clive certainly did as he helped me down. Afterwards at dinner parties, he used to joke that seeing me like that almost made up for missing Botham make the winning century.

I feel so culpable (is that the right word?) for making you fall. If I hadn't written that rather starchy letter, you wouldn't have been running upstairs at all. Lesley's yoga teacher says that negative energy is bound to beget negative results, and I must say now that I've had proof positive. I am going to buy one of those ionisers to see if that will charge the atmosphere at home in a more constructive way, and also between you and me, I'm going to stop taking the tablets the doctor prescribed – they make me feel so depressed.

I hope you are enjoying the flowers I sent – I asked for a mixture of yellow – always such a cheering colour I feel – so I hope they followed my instructions. The girl at the florist's *looked* as if she'd understood me, but you never can tell.

9

Incidentally, just to put the record straight, I did enjoy your chocolate square recipe. I said it was rich because I was angry, but in actual fact I gorged the whole lot myself the evening that Lesley and Keith returned from their honeymoon, so I've only got myself to blame for being sick afterwards.

I do hope you're feeling a little bit better now, and look forward to hearing from you.

With kindest regards for a speedy recovery,

Irene

27th August

Dear Irene,

Thank you for the kind letter. You are a silly to think that I blame you in any way for the fall. I'm sure I never intended to give that impression and I feel terrible that you have been lacerating yourself about it. The flowers were lovely by the way, sweetpeas in pink and mauve – I always think they are so uretheal looking, though of course, they don't last. Mabel had to clear them out by the time I returned from my few days away. Did you get my P.C.? Mabel didn't receive hers until two days after I was back. I don't know what they do with all those twenty pees. You might as well send stuff by carrier pigeon!

In case you didn't, an old friend of mine, Audrey Roscoe, runs a little guest house nearby on the coast, and I popped off there for a few days recuperation. I must say I *was* made a fuss of. Audrey is a great one for chat – in fact most nights my head was ringing by the time we got to bed, and on the Tuesday I went down with an awful migraine – but all the cooking was done by hand, and the views from her bay window are quite panamaric. Of course it rained like a drain the whole time, but I just put on my old boots and waterproof jerkin and strode off across the pebbles. I don't care what anyone says, sea air does make you feel better – you should try it. Nothing drives the 'blues' away quicker than a brisk walk in a howling gale. I was quite sorry to have to come back and pick up the 'threads' again. Mabel had got me in one or two provisions, which was very kind, although she will buy that Longlife milk and she knows I can't stand it. But you should have seen the pile of bills (Gerald always used to call it 'hate' mail) awaiting my return! Also a tile had come off the roof and water had poured into the attic onto my old sewing machine, which I believe is quite a collector's item these days. Sometimes you wonder if it's worth it!

How are Lesley and Keith? You hardly mention them in your last. Any holiday snaps? I'd love to see them and the wedding ones if it isn't too much bother. I found a couple of petals in the pocket of that two-piece I wore. I believe they are off your hat! Do you want them back? They are rather crumpled, I'm afraid!

Best regards,

Vera

Dear Irene,

Having a few blowy days down by the sea. Hobbled as far as the front for these p.c.'s but I'm all done in after a few yards. Could hardly make it to the ladies conveniences – now I know how the dog feels! Audrey has just kicked me up with Jack the Ripper and a steaming hot mug of Bovril

Best Wishes,
Vera

Irene Spencer

34 Wormwold Way

Hethergreen

'Spumy Sea', photo by Craig Douglas.

13

28th August

Dear Vera,

I am glad to hear you have had a rest and are on the road to recovery, and *what* a coincidence that you know Audrey Roscoe. I knew her some long time ago before she moved to the coast, and never quite took to her. You are absolutely right when you say she's a chatterer – mostly rather catty gossip unfounded on fact, I seem to remember. Although I'm sure she wouldn't remember me.

Don't bother returning the petals – I shall never use that hat again as a hat. I shall snip the remaining blooms off and use them as the central theme for my Yuletide table decoration. It'll be nice to remember the wedding at Christmas. Lesley should be about ready for some home cooking then! I've hardly seen them since they've been back – they must be so busy settling in. Of course she doesn't want my help; she has to do everything by herself. Oh well, I suppose I was the same when I was first married, until I learnt that a mother really *is* a girl's best friend. Unfortunately my own mother passed away shortly after I'd learnt to appreciate her, a tragedy that I have regretted bitterly ever since.

Well, cheerio for now, I shall have to get on. I've got to pop into the village to get one or two essentials, and I shall go into the florist while I'm down there and give her a piece of my mind. That's the second time she's got the order wrong, and it just isn't good enough. She made my memorial tribute to Clive a sheaf instead of a wreath, and I'd expressly said in the *Chronicle* 'no cut flowers'. I'm sure his sister Doreen still thinks it was done on purpose to draw attention to myself.

The postman's just delivered your postcard. I've never cared much for that part of the country – it's so flat and insipid isn't it? What a shame the weather was so dreadful! Still, a change is as good as a rest. Take care of yourself and don't overdo things.

Kind regards,

Irene

September 10th

Dear Irene,

I've been so busy since I got back what with the garden – the lawn was full of moss – and the bottling season, that it's a pleasure to have only to sit down and write a letter. I am looking out onto a glorious sunset (one of the best features of a picture window) and a haze of blue smoke. At first I thought the house was on fire, but then I realised they were just burning the stubble in the neighbouring fields. This part of the country is so picturesque in the Autumn. I have been jamming and pickling like a lunatic. Six pounds of Gooseberry, four of Bramble Jelly, three of Greengage, and some Pear and Walnut Chutney. I love an oriental recipe. Really, it is silly to do so much – last year's is still in the larder, but it's such a hard habit to break isn't it, doing things for a *family*?

I am hoping Karen will come for Christmas so she can take some back. Actually I'm a bit worried about her. She's gone terribly faddy with her food, won't eat meat and goes berserk about chemical additives. I hope she doesn't count pectin, or I shall have to take the lot to the Bring and Buy! Howard never notices what he's eating – just like a man! – so he's easy to please. Must close now. Mabel Thrush has been rather poorly and the Vicar is going to pop in shortly. She got in an awful fluster about him seeing the state of the place (she's a bit of a fanatic for the Hoover), so I have had to clean all her brass and make a Battenburg for tea.

Yours in haste,

Vera

P.S. I'm so glad the card arrived. I was afraid the GPO
would make me out a liar. Fancy you knowing Audrey! She
did mention you as a matter of fact, but I always take
everything she says with a pinch of salt.

October 3rd

Dear Irene,

I have been in such a state since I last wrote that it has taken me all this time to realise I have not had a reply to my last. I am so worried. Are you ill, or has some kind of crisis occurred? Do put me out of my anxiety with a note – however brief. I am up to my eyes in plaster dust and rubble. I feel rather like a victim of the Mexico City Earthquake. The builders are in. They came to replace a tile in the roof, but one of them put his foot through the ceiling and brought the lot down. They had to take up the carpet, and then discovered some beetle in a floorboard. Too late I discovered I am allergic to woodworm spray, and am now attending outpatients for chronic asthma and staying with Mabel Thrush. Write to me at home – I pop in once a day to collect the mail and wrench a few more artyfacts out of the debris.

Yours affec.,

Vera

October 7th

Dear Vera,

I'm so sorry not to have corresponded before now, and to get you into a tizz. I am absolutely fine thank you, so there is no cause for concern. I do hope you are more organised with the builders now. Personally I always pay that little bit extra and get a reputable firm. It saves time and money in the long run.

To be quite frank, I didn't write at first because of my annoyance over Audrey Roscoe. I bet I know what she said about me, and it has very little basis in truth. Clive was very drunk at the time, and didn't know what he was doing, and anyway I was on holiday. But I don't know why I'm bothering to go into it. It's all in the past and that sort of woman isn't worth the paper and ink.

Anyway, that isn't the main reason why I didn't write, only the first reason, which I soon got over, and am completely over now. In fact if you see her again, do please give her my kindest regards, and tell her I hope her son is better now. He went to prison you know – did she tell you? I think that's why she moved so far away.

I can't write much more just now, because Bill is coming over to take me out to a dinner dance. Life has been so hectic since he has been paying his attentions, and I must say it has perked me up no end. He is a widower, and an old friend of Clive's and mine. His wife died very slowly and painfully last year, and I have never seen a man so devoted. Actually he was at Lesley's wedding. You may remember him. He wore a grey morning suit, where most of the men wore tails. I'm sure you'd like him very much. He is what used to be called a gentleman.

Actually, most Sundays we go out for a run in his car, and I have been thinking of suggesting that we drive over to see you. It's just a suggestion of course, and I quite understand if you're too busy. Bill says he knows an exquisite French restaurant quite near Little Potterton – he knows the owners very well – and he says he would be delighted to take us both there for Sunday lunch. Would you enjoy that? Life can be so lonely on your own, I know. Anyway, I'll leave it with you and wait until you get in touch, but the first and third Sundays in November would be fine with us.

Do take care of your asthma. There's nothing worse than a nasty chest.

Fondest wishes,

Irene

October 20th

Dear Irene,

How pleasant to hear from you at last. I am so glad you haven't allowed your new 'interest' to completely take over your life. I always think people live to regret abandoning old friends when new ones appear – particularly as one can never be certain how long these things will last. I do indeed remember 'Bill' from the reception. He was the one who dropped the Salmon Mousse all down his front wasn't he? I remember he swore rather loudly – I assumed because his suit was hired. How nice that he has a car to take you around in. You know, you really should have learned to drive, there is no substitute for independent wheels. The times I have driven off and left Gerald pissed as a fart at some Round Table do or other!

Do by all means come over and see me one Sunday, though I can't recommend the restaurant you mention. It's called 'Les Liaisons Dangereuses' and I must say their menu bears the name out. *I* certainly wouldn't put a Strawberry Pernod sauce with Halibut!

However if you would like to sample some less reshershe dishes at my humble abode, I'd be delighted. It would have to be the 3rd Sunday as the first is the Blood Donors Remembrance Service, and I always do the flowers.

Best wishes,

Vera

P.S. My chest is much better. Mabel Thrush knitted me a thermal boob tube.

21

November 29th

Dear Vera,

Just a little 'thank you' note for such a pleasant day! It was lovely to see you after all this writing – you looked quite different to how I remembered, although of course you were just the same as your letters.

The lunch was superb! I've always admired people who cook in an exotic way. Personally I am a plain cook, but then so many men say that is what they like, don't they? I know Clive did. Anyway, Bill thought it was absolutely gorgeous, and on a par with 'Les Liaisons Dangerous'.

I was so pleased that the two of you got on. It's so nice when one's friends like each other isn't it? He thought you were lovely, very attractive. He's not stopped going on about how nice you looked in that two-piece you had on from Marks. He wanted me to buy one, but I think that style would drown me, don't you? When you're slim and fine-boned, you have to be very careful what you wear.

I'm so pleased to have seen your 'cottage' – how quaint! Now I can imagine you in your setting when I write.

What are you doing at Christmas? Is Karen coming home? I'm still hoping that Lesley and Keith will come here, but they still haven't committed themselves. Still, I daresay Bill will want to see me over the holidays, so it may be just as well if they don't come.

Anyway, must close, I'm running out of space on the notelet. Thank you once again for the lovely day. Bill said he would be writing to you himself, but I'll thank you from us both anyway. You know what men are like! You must come here soon.

Fond regards,

Irene

December 10th

Dearest Irene,

Forgive me for being a while in answering. It has been all go here since Mabel Thrush went into hospital. Did I mention that she had to have her leg off? I have just come back from visiting now. She had run out of two-ply Heliotrope and Lemon Barley water. I said to myself, that puts paid to her having the dog again, she'll never be able to take it 'walkies'. Some people will go to any lengths to avoid being neighbourly!

Talking of the dog, I do apologise for her behaviour when you visited – she really doesn't usually make that awful 'pong'. She gets nervous when strangers are in the house. As for her trying to climb onto Bill's lap – well! I had to laugh afterwards when I thought of the two of them struggling with the seat belt! Did you have a good journey back? I thought Bill was a trifle 'one over the eight'! He's written me a very nice note as a matter of fact. Funnily enough he's going to be in this area over the break, visiting some relations – do you know them? Perhaps he will bring you with him and we can all meet up for a glass of Christmas cheer. I must say I am at a loss over Christmas – Karen still hasn't said a word – I suppose it will depend upon the state of her 'relationship'. Howard is going to walk the 'Pennine Way' with a friend. Seems a peculiar way to spend Christmas to me. I don't know whether to get food in or not. I suppose I will have to have Mabel in for Boxing Day, but frankly I'm not getting a huge bird just for me and her and the dog. I shall just depend on my deep-freeze.

I suppose you will be 'gadding' with Bill when the holiday season starts. How lovely to have some reasons for dressing up. I haven't worn my diamanté since the night Gerald died. By the way I *loved* that tweed suit you were

23

wearing. So comfy looking and warm. Would you call that colour Biscuit? Don't take any notice of Bill – you've got your own taste and style, most definitely.

I'm off to do some Christmas shopping now so I will close. Do drop me a line before the awful whirl takes over. I don't know about you, but the sight of Yule logs and tinselled cribs fills me with horror these days.

Love

Vera

P.S. What an awful thing to say about Mabel – I do hope you realised it was only a joke!

22nd December

Dear Vera,

I hope this parcel gets to you for Christmas Day at this short notice. It's just a small token – an offcut I picked up in the market, and just hand-rolled the edges, but I know it looks expensive. I was going to give you a couple of my pewter goblets as well, since I've got eight, and I never have more than six round my table now. But I'm not going to send them through the post – it'd cost a fortune.

I'm disappointed at not seeing you at Christmas, but it's my own fault for just assuming and not asking. When Bill mentioned yesterday that it was his mother-in-law he'd be staying with, I immediately understood that it would be quite improper for me to go with him. If I'd only known before, I daresay I could have stayed with you, but only finding out three days before Christmas, I couldn't have imposed.

Anyway, it doesn't matter. I've had to do emergency shopping today, since I hadn't expected to be doing any catering, and quite frankly I am exhausted. I am sitting in Grey's Coffee Lounge at the moment, writing to you prior to wrapping and posting and tracking down some sausage meat. Lesley and Keith, of course, had already arranged to spend Christmas with his parents, but now they're all coming over to me for Boxing Day tea, so it's only me for Christmas dinner, but I would miss the sausage in the stuffing.

Anyway, must get on. There's a queue of people for tables, and I can't spin this coffee out any longer. Have a lovely Christmas. I shouldn't be surprised if you see Bill – he took your telephone number with him and said he might look you up. If you do, wish him a happy Christmas from me. Obviously I can't phone him while he's away. Although

I suppose that if he did visit you, he could phone me from your phone. You could tell him to reverse the charges. And it would be nice of course to speak to you too.

Anyway, it's just an idea. Must go now, the waitress is getting edgy. Perhaps hear from you in the near future.

Kindest regards,

Irene

2nd January

Dear Irene,

I am so glad you made that unexpected visit on Christmas Day, even if you did find me up to my elbows in Sage and Onion. How lucky your friends happened to be driving up this way. I do hope the day was pleasanter for you than it was for me. Frankly I was in that much of a fluster with Karen just descending out of the blue, and Bill dropping by at 9.30 on Christmas morning for a sherry, I didn't know whether I was coming or going! Judging by the shade of my face when I finally had a moment to apply some lipstick, I must have been half cut. Bill's hand slipped with the sherry bottle! I did find it empty in the dustbin later. What a shame you missed him.

Boxing Day was much nicer. Bill took us for a run in the afternoon. We went up to look at the new Nuclear Power plant. Actually Karen refused to come. She and Bill had words over South Africa when we were eating our Stilton and grapes (I had stupidly left the Outspan sticker on with the price, but really, she needn't have drawn attention!) Karen was in a towering rage the whole of the holiday. When I asked her what was wrong she nearly bit my head off. She and Kevin are having a 'Trial Separation', but she only found out on Christmas Eve.

Bill was very upset he'd missed you. He said you were a stupid prat not to have phoned him – his mother-in-law is as deaf as a post. We did have a laugh!

I feel quite flat now they've all gone home. Kevin rang on New Year's Day and said the trial was over. Karen said she supposed he had emptied the deep-freeze by now. She left this morning with half the turkey. I shall fricassee the rest and take it round to Mabel. She *would* come out on New Year's Eve. I was going to a 'do' at the Undertakers' Hall (they always have such glorious flower arrangements) but of course I felt I had to stay with Mabel. I saw the New Year in with a glass of Lucozade. Mabel drank her denture water by mistake.

Well – toodlepip and Happy New Year. Bill said I must pop down and see you both again soon – he even mentioned a holiday cottage weekend.

All the best,

Vera

Two Years Later

28th April

Dear Vera,

I was clearing out my drawers this morning and I came across your letters, and quite frankly I haven't had a moment's peace since. I thought to myself, well, you've got two options, either chuck them out and put it out of your mind, or screw up your courage and write to her. Well as you can see, I opted for the latter – I couldn't put it out of my mind at all. I've been plunged into soul-searching and depression all day, it just raked it all back up. When I think back now, I feel really stupid and ashamed and if I had my time over again, the whole silly episode wouldn't have been allowed to come to a head. But there you are, it did, and what's done can't be undone. Looking back on it now I think that if only I'd kept my cool and laughed it off (as I notice Marjorie Proops recommended to a girl this week in the *Mirror* who was in a situation similar to mine) then the whole thing would probably have blown over and nothing would have come of it. Anyway, it's no use crying over spilt milk, and we can all be wise after the event.

I don't even know if you're still at the same address, but if you do get this and decide to reply, I'd be overjoyed to hear how you are. I'm still at the same place. I don't think I'll ever move now – I couldn't face the upheaval. Lesley's had a little girl and they're thinking of going to Australia.

All for now in case you're not there. I don't want all my news falling into the wrong hands.

With sincere good wishes,

Irene Spencer

6th May

Dear Irene,

I was so pleased to get your letter, I felt at last that I'd been 'forgiven'. I can't tell you how many anguished sleepless nights I've had over the whole thing – so much so that the Doctor had to put me on medication. He said if I went on the way I was doing I would certainly end up in a neck brace. Of course, that fall didn't help – I still have terrible trouble with my lesions. It took me several months to climb out of the 'Slough of Despond', and I was very much aided by literature and music. I've cleaned the library out of Barbara Taylor Bradford, and found Strauss particularly cheering. In fact there was one amusing occasion when the glazier came to replace the picture window and found me waltzing with a moss pole! There weren't many 'highs' however in the months that followed that incident.

Speaking of which, I want to put your mind at rest once and for all about one thing. Bill and I never meant to end up in bed together. It was all a mistake on the part of the hotel receptionist, who was a deputy stand-in for the Bank Holiday. The hotel did apologise profusely when they saw the trouble they'd caused. They were certainly impressed when Bill hauled the assistant manager over the counter and threatened to unpick his hairweave.

I *did* think the suite was rather palatial when I was shown up, but it was late and I was tired, so I went straight into the adjoining bathroom and started to undress. Unbeknownst to me, Bill was doing the same thing in *his* adjoining bathroom. There are two in the Honeymoon Suite, you see, I suppose to avoid disappointment. I came out in my nightie, got into bed, put out the light and dozed off without even Barbara Cartland. Bill must have done the same – we never noticed each other, which of course is easily done in a king-size. Imagine how we felt, when suddenly the light snapped on and there were you with your suitcase! Now I *know* what it must have looked like with Bill wrapped round me like a Russian vine. As he said to me afterwards, he thought I was a bolster – but I don't think that was any reason for you to storm out and refuse to discuss it. I mean, put yourself in my position, in bed with a stranger and without a scrap of make-up. You weren't the only one in shock! Bill gave his knee a terrible wrench leaping out to follow you and goodness knows what the porter made of a man in pyjama bottoms hopping on one foot through the foyer. It wasn't until a week later that it struck me as odd that you'd booked the Honeymoon Suite to begin with. Bill was as mystified as I was. He was under the impression that it was a weekend break for three singles.

I can't deny that it did lead to a greater intimacy between Bill and myself (there's something so endearing about seeing a man in agony) but that went the way of all things, including the picture window.

All I can say is I'm as willing as you are to pick up the pieces. Mabel Thrush is dead, as is the dog, and life can be awfully lonely.

Yours,

Vera

14th May

Dear Vera,

Thank you for your letter, my dear. Although I have no
intention of raking up the past, your letter brought it all
back – and of course, told me some things I didn't know –
and my first reaction upon reading it was to get in a rage all
over again, which I can ill afford with *my* blood pressure, as
Dr Prior-Palmer is always pointing out. It's all very well
saying don't worry so much and relax, but I've never got to
the bottom of how he thinks this is supposed to be done.
Anyway.

I did *not* book the Honeymoon Suite. In fact, as Bill well
knew at the time, I did not do the booking at all – he did. Or
rather his secretary probably did, since as far as I could see
he never made a phone call he could avoid, and certainly
never *dialled* himself. I remember wondering if he had a
septic finger, or if it was a phobia? So *what*, you may ask,
was he up to? I have puzzled it over, and can only come up
with answers too far-fetched to contemplate. Still. You may
say it's all water under the bridge, and I would be the first to
agree, particularly as Bill married a girl half his age last year
and is now a father again. At his time in life! His son is
younger than any of his grandchildren – he's been bragging
about it at the golf club, and pretending he's over the moon,
but they tell me he looks absolutely haggard. Apparently
she's a Women's Libber. Serve him right.

Anyway, I didn't write this letter to talk about him. How
are *you*? I'm so sorry to hear about Mabel. You sound a bit
down in the mouth. I am free next weekend and the
weekend after. Why don't you come on a visit? It would be
so pleasant to see you again and discuss old times – well,
some of them. Anyway, let me know your plans and we'll fix
the arrangements.

With all best wishes and kindest regards,

Irene

P.S. I've re-read your letter – what's all this about the picture window going west? Surely not? The best thing about your living room is being able to see out.

16th May

Dear Irene,

I can't come this weekend as it's over to Great Potterton for their Bring and Buy for the disabled, but I could come the weekend after. How about if I came on the Wednesday and stayed till the Tuesday? I'd have to be back then as it's my Scientific and Geographical Society on the 31st, and we're having a talk about Scottish heather. Oh, look at me rushing on and I haven't even said thank you for the kind invitation. Of *course* I'd be glad to keep you company – I'm sure it's very depressing having time on your hands on a Sunday. Did you say Lesley had gone to Australia? Karen and Kevin have split up, did I mention? Karen said finding the crab was the last straw. I don't know to which crab she was referring. Children can be such a worry, especially if they're far away! I haven't seen Howard since he went to live in the country – some village he and his friend found when they walked the Pennine Way. When he told me he was going to Derbyshire I thought he meant for the weekend, not for two years.

Well, must finish as I've got to get 'stuck in' to my gâteaux and fancies for the Bring and Buy. I always do the tea and I pride myself on a glorious spread. Last year I made fifteen puddings. Several are still in the deep-freeze.

See you, all being well, on the 25th.

Warmest regards,

Vera

P.S. The picture window is a long story and I won't bore you with it now, except to say I was very disappointed. I had always understood reinforced glass was supposed to withstand the heaviest of flung objects.

36

18th May

Dear Vera,

By all means come on the 25th. I've spent the morning on the phone rejigging my arrangements, and have managed to clear the whole six days, so don't worry, my time is yours. If you want to come by train I can pick you up from the station – I took my driving test last year, and passed with flying colours. I don't know why Clive always told me it was so difficult. Anyway, give me a ring if you want picking up, and I'll be at the station with a red carpet!

Looking forward to catching up,

Best regards,

Irene

20th May

Dear Irene,

I *shall* come on the train as Karen wrote off my car on
Saturday. She rang me from a lay-by to say she'd had a little
'prang' as she called it, and could I get the AA out to help
her. Well, needless to say I couldn't get through to them,
and ended up going to fetch her myself in my neighbour's
farm truck. I was half way down the motorway before I
realised it still had the combine harvester attached. When I
looked at the car I could have wept. Completely stoved in
from bonnet to boot! Mercifully Karen was alive, though
frankly that was a situation I could cheerfully have altered. I
suppose it was silly of me to get so upset, as Karen said to
me as she dragged me, sobbing, back onto the hard
shoulder, 'Oh for God's sake, mother, it's only a car, claim
on the bloody insurance!' But to me that little Fiesta was
like family. I was closer to it than I've ever been to Karen.
I'm intimate with its internal structure for a start. Anyway. I
shall be arriving on the 3.45 on Wednesday. Never mind the
red carpet, but have a gin and tonic ready!

Looking forward immensely to seeing you,

All the best till then,

Vera

21st May

Dear Vera,

I'd just nipped down to the village to get some gin after receiving your letter – I don't normally keep it in – when I suddenly remembered the Cricket Club Ladies Night Dance on Friday. Being the widow of an ex-Vice Captain I am of course expected to attend, and this year I have been chosen to judge the Spot Prize, so I can't let them down. I raced round to see Arthur Snushall, who organises it all and was a great friend of Clive's, and explained the dilemma still clutching the bottle of gin, I realised afterwards, so I don't know what he made of that, and the upshot of it was that he said he'd be delighted to have an extra spare lady so you're welcome to come. I hope to goodness that you get this in time to organise a long dress as it is formal. I'm in the post office and I'm holding up Mrs Bickerton so I'd better close.

See you Wednesday!

Irene

1st June

My very dear Irene,

Well, here I am back in 'casa mia' and feeling very 'down in the dumps'. Words are inadequate (they so frequently *are* aren't they?) to express my thanks for such a splendidly enjoyable time. I've often thought penning an Opera the only really satisfactory way of expressing great emotion. Sadly I am not gifted in that direction, though Karen once rudely remarked that I lived my life as though it were one. Which reminds me, you're a dark horse, keeping quiet about that nice young curate Bruce until he appeared at Sunday lunchtime! That was a merry gathering wasn't it? I do hope he was alright for Evensong. I don't care what people say about 'High' or 'Low'; the clergy should always be accessible. He reminded me of Gideon, a young man I was once in love with. He took me to the tennis club New Year's Eve dance and we made many revelations to each other in the back of his Baby Austin. The next day he dropped in a note informing me he was taking Holy Orders. Of course, I was very young myself at the time – this was 1937.

What a charmer Arthur Snushall is! He apologised so profusely, I don't know how you have the heart to still be angry with him. It was an honest mistake and easily made when you are three sheets to the wind, or perhaps, in Arthur's case, three and a half. I thoroughly enjoyed presenting the prize, even though the winning couple had stepped on my fishtail (thank heavens I still have the use of Mabel Thrush's Singer) and I was quite at a loss with the jokes about legside wides and maiden overs. Gerald wasn't a cricket player.

In fact all your friends were very hospitable and pleasant. I don't know why you warned me about Dorothy Bickerstaff.

She had nothing but kind words to say about you, including that Clive had led you a dog's life and you'd made an amazing recovery. Your cooking was ... well, what can I say? *Prolific.* Don't forget to put in that recipe for the mulled wine – your curate certainly enjoyed it! Oh dear, the phone is ringing ...

That was Karen. Apparently she is coming on a visit. She *never* comes this time of year – it's always August for my birthday, or Christmas. She was as brief as ever. As soon as I said I'd be there to meet the train, she slammed down the receiver. I *do* hope ... oh well, never mind. Better close now as I must scurry round and get some food in, also remember to put up the picture she gave me last Christmas and remove Kevin from the wedding photo.

With a million thanks,

Toodlepip,

Vera

P.S. I've just thought what the opera would be called – of course, 'The Merry Widow'!

4th June

Dear Vera,

You may not be aware that my maiden name was Onions. When I was a child I tried to honour my father and my mother who sacrificed everything for my education at Tavistock Road School for Girls, by working hard and trying to excel, despite the fact that I have never been a top notch intellectual. I am sure that you can imagine my gratified delight therefore when in my last year, after striving for recognition for so long, I was awarded an inscribed and beautifully bound copy of the King James Bible for Neatness. I can remember to this day the pride with which I took my place on the platform to receive it from Miss Frobisher herself in my darned but immaculate school uniform, and for the occasion, a borrowed pair of white kid gloves. The school hall resounded with cheers, and I was happier then than I have ever been. On returning to my place however, pressed by the girls to show them my award, I opened the book at the inscribed plate only to see not my name but Irene Springthorpe's, the girl who had head lice in 4B. On being informed of the reason for my distress, Miss Frobisher assured me it was an obvious error, and offered to have it scratched out and amended, but as it was a prize for neatness I naturally declined. They say that pride comes before a fall, but in my case it was simultaneous. Even though I look at that bible every day, I can never open it without being filled with a sense of cruel injustice.

The handing out of the Spot Prizes this year at the Ladies Night Dinner Dance was to have been an honour bestowed upon me by the Club in recognition of my doing the catering for the players' refreshment for twenty-five years, and carrying on to this day despite my husband not playing for the team after he died three years ago. I can forgive Arthur his mistake, since as he said himself he was wearing the wrong glasses, but I find it very difficult to come to terms with your selfishness in not pointing it out, and just capitalising on it to hog the limelight.

Another thing you might be amused by is that your friend Dorothy Bickerstaff has every reason to say that Clive led me a dog's life, considering she was the bitch who led him astray when Lesley was teething and I had temporarily let myself go. Trust you to like her. You are so easily taken in.

As for your allegations about Bruce and myself, I can assure you that our relations go no further than his kind offer to help me out over a couple of sticky points in St Paul's Epistle to the Ephesians. When he came round this morning and found me crying tears of rage over your letter, he pointed out to me St Paul's wisdom (Ch. 4, v. 26) 'Let not the sun go down upon your wrath', so you've got him to thank that I have taken the trouble to write you this response, to give you the opportunity of apologising. Left to my own devices I would more probably have followed the teaching in verse 27, 'Neither give place to the devil', and just severed our connection. Incidentally, Bruce is an unswerving teetotal, so if your memory of Sunday's lunch is that he was enjoying my mulled wine in a ribald manner, I think it wiser not to enclose the recipe. Perhaps you are trying to model yourself too closely on 'The Merry Widow'? I trust you will take this letter in the spirit it is intended, and that you will try to have more thought for others instead of sailing gaily through their lives, treading on their corns.

Kind regards,

Irene

12th June

Dear Irene,

I hardly know how to respond to your last. I had no idea I was giving such offence. My 'jokey' tone was an attempt (misplaced I now see) to jolly you out of the doldrums you were in during the latter half of my visit. I'm sure a little harmless teasing cannot alone have produced this response and can only think there is something else going on of a 'personal' nature ... perhaps involving that nice young curate ...? By the by, I certainly didn't mean to imply that he was a toper, not that that in itself would be unusual in the cloth. The vicar who married Gerald and myself could hardly stand up – if it comes to that neither could Gerald – and was seen at the reception with a bottle of sherry under one arm and a bridesmaid under the other. But I digress ...

On re-reading your letter, I'm reminded of the dreadful time that I fell out with my (ex) best friend Muriel. She was convinced I was 'after' her boyfriend, which was utter nonsense. It was all a mistake, which came about when I wore one of her frocks to a party. She didn't speak to me for a month and I was so upset I actually contemplated suicide and went as far as an overdose of my mother's indigestion tablets. Thirteen is such an emotive age isn't it?

I *am* sorry about your awful childhood. It excuses a lot. I told myself again how lucky I was – my father may have been tyrannical but he was a natural musician. And of course I was always at the centre of a group of friends and admirers. Speaking of which, Eric Glendower is coming up the path so I must finish this later ...

He wanted me to sponsor him for a swim. I said yes, as I'm sure he'll never go over three lengths – his pacemaker couldn't take it. Last week Mavis Peake cost me an arm and a leg on a sponsored ice dance for pensioners. Actually she cost herself an arm and a leg also – during the rhumba she fell over and broke her wrist and her ankle. It's been a week for breakages – Karen dropped my best Denbighware casserole on the floor on Sunday and scattered it and its contents, (Chicken à la King) to the four winds … or perhaps I should say, the four walls – I scraped most of it off the paintwork. She said I made her jump, but I ask you, if you can't go into your own kitchen without knocking, where can you go?! I didn't say anything. The fact is she was jumpy as a cat all weekend. She's obviously got something on her mind, but I'll be the last to know it.

Well my dear, I do hope this has put the record straight between us. I'm sure in a saner moment you will realize how highly I value our friendship. As I said to Karen at the weekend, I had no idea women could be so close. At last I know what it is to have a sister. She gave me her usual scornful glance and said where had I been for the last twenty years – had I *heard* of the women's movement?

Hoping you feel better soon,

Very best wishes,

Vera

20th June

Dear Vera,

Where are you? I've been trying to phone and you're *never* in. I have been living under a cloud for weeks, and now the worst has happened. Keith got the job he was after in Wollongong, New South Wales. Right up until the last minute I thought he wouldn't get it – I know for a fact that his spelling is shocking, but apparently that is what secretaries are for and it doesn't seem to matter in top jobs if you are illiterate or not. It was touch and go up to the last minute as there was a chap from Huddersfield they really wanted more than Keith, but then he found out he was HIVES positive so he didn't want to leave his family. What sort of a company is it who would be taken in by a man like that in the first place? Anyway by the time they'd sorted all that lot out everything had to happen at once, and Lesley and Keith left yesterday and took my baby girl. What sort of a country is that to bring a child up in?

When I think of all we sacrificed for Lesley – years ago Clive could have taken a very well paid job in Croydon, London, but we didn't take it because we didn't want her growing up a street urchin in a big city. How will they ever find a baby sitter that they can trust? The stories you read in the papers today, you can't trust anybody outside the family to look after your children, and even inside the family it seems there is a minefield of danger if there are male members. I won't see her grow up, and by the time I get to see her again she'll be talking with that dreadful accent.

And there was never any question of them asking me what I thought, or of asking me to go with them. I shouldn't have gone anyway, as I think young people have to be left alone to make their own mistakes. I could cheerfully throttle Lesley, and I know if Clive had been alive he'd have knocked their heads together. And what about her schooling? Her qualifications won't be worth the paper they're written on. And what about when she gets ill? Would *you* like to be operated on by a foreign doctor? I know I wouldn't. And what about eating? The food will all be different, and Cheryl Marie is so faddy, and with Lesley for a mother she'll have faded to nothing before she notices.

I'm absolutely beside myself and I've been sobbing for days. I think there ought to be a law against people taking the children out of the family. Wilfully wicked and adulterous parents are allowed rights, but you never hear about the rights of the grandparents, which is ridiculous when you think that all of the Law Lords must be grandparents themselves. Not to see my baby grow up is the cruellest thing Lesley could ever do to me, and she's done some things in her time. When she went to college it had to be the other end of the country.

And I'm just supposed to clean up the mess. They've left me with her house to sell, and I've to arrange shipment of various bits of furniture. Why couldn't Lesley have stayed to do that herself? And how irresponsible for the three of them to fly out on the same plane – you'd never catch the Royal family doing that, and let's face it, they are seasoned air travellers.

I've just tried ringing you again but you're still not answering. It's five a.m. and it's too late to go to bed now. I couldn't sleep anyway, despite the brandy I've taken to dull my emotion. I have never felt so alone. I am even questioning whether there is a God, which I am sure Bruce could put my mind at rest on if he wasn't on a retreat in the Holy Lands. Please come and help me out Vera, I really need a friend and you know I don't ask for favours lightly.

My brandy glass has just shattered in my hand for no apparent reason, hence the blood on the first page. Everything is going against me. I'd ring the Samaritans but I don't know their number. Lesley just rang, bubbling over, to say they'd arrived safely. She seems incapable of grasping the fact that if I'd been asleep she'd have woken me up. I suppose now I'm going to have to face years of sleepless nights wondering if she's going to ring. She wouldn't put Cheryl Marie to the phone, but I could hear crying in the background. I knew she wouldn't be happy there. What can I do?

Yours in distress,

Irene

24th June

My dear Irene,

I nearly wept when I read your letter. To be honest, I had
plenty to weep about. You couldn't get me as I was away,
looking after Karen. I was rung up in the middle of the night
last Tuesday by some hospital orderly saying they'd found
my name in Karen's Filofax under 'Next of kin' (3rd after
Auntie Madge who's dead and Uncle Dick who's an
alcoholic) and could I come immediately? Of course I
jumped straight to the conclusion that she'd been in a
frightful accident, aided by the orderly, who told me she was
dying. Turned out he'd said *crying*, but the combination of
middle of the night confusion and foreign accent had me
running to the car and driving all the way to the hospital,
exceeding the speed limit and wearing my reading glasses. I
have only once before covered ground so fast and that was
on a pair of out of control skis in the Cairngorms.

The hospital was in semi-darkness (I believe they are
economising on electricity – couldn't get a cup of tea for
love nor money) and a very junior night-nurse eventually
located Karen for me, not, thank God, in the mortuary, but
in the Margaret Hilda Roberts ward, a desolate room empty
but for a single bed and a do-it-yourself First Aid kit. Karen
was asleep and was not very pleased when I shook her
awake. She said what on earth was I doing there, and when I
told her I'd been summoned she snorted something about
'bloody stupid red tape' and turned over. It was hours
before I could get any further information, or indeed a cup
of tea.

I don't know if I dare tell you the rest. Oh Irene, what a
blessing it is that you're such a good friend … and so far
away. If I confided this to anyone here, it would be round

49

the village in seconds. Karen finally told me the truth. She is pregnant.

I had to stop and have a stiff whisky. I don't know what's the matter with me, I must be in shock. I'd describe my symptoms as menopausal, if all that weren't far behind me. In fact Karen didn't tell me, the ward sister did when she came on duty next morning. She explained that Karen had been rushed to hospital with a suspected miscarriage. They'd needed to give her a blood transfusion and as they didn't have any handy, they'd phoned next of kin (me) to see if I could donate some. I was rolling up my sleeve when she said not to worry, they'd found some frozen in the canteen fridge and they were confident that would do her.

I can't describe to you my horror, rage, despair, etc. I had no idea. As you know, Karen has been estranged from her husband for over two years now. They *have* met on occasion, but only with a solicitor present.

I sat with her until she came to again, but I couldn't bring myself to touch her. When she woke up her first question was whether she'd lost the baby. I said unfortunately not, but we'd just have to grin and bear it. She told me not to be so F-word stupid, she wanted the baby desperately and was delighted she hadn't miscarried. I'm afraid I lost my temper and shouted at her. I don't know what I said. Years of pent-up grief came out, starting with the time, aged three, she'd smashed a doll I'd had since *I* was a baby. She just stared at me and when I dried up said I'd better make use of my hospital trip to visit the psychiatrist. I retorted that I hoped the blood transfusion hadn't been infected, but in any case the baby would probably have hooves as it had come from a pound of calves liver. The awful things one says in the heat of the moment! Of course she broke down and cried and then the sister came along and said they needed the bed and could I take her home now? That's where I've been ever since.

I'm so wrapped up in my own anguished misery, I've got nothing left over for other people. I can't face going out of doors and certainly couldn't stand the strain of travelling on public transport. You are welcome to come to me my dear and I'll do my best to cheer you, but I feel I must warn you to be prepared for a sorry wrung out dishcloth.

Yours, as ever,

Vera

4th July

Dear Vera,

The journey back was the worst in living memory. I had
to stand all the way to Crowick while 'businessmen' had
seats paid for by their companies for the tax relief. I have
torn up my Pensioners Railcard and have sent half to the
Ministry of Transport and half to Mrs Thatcher, with
covering letters demanding a refund and reminding them
that it was people like me who voted them in. Never again! I
feel quite 'militant' after my talks with Karen, and will
certainly be writing more letters of a complaining nature in
future. The only nice part of the return itinerary was a most
charming West Indian bus conductor who has just joined
our 41 bus route at home, and who helped me with my
case. I'm very much looking forward to travelling with him
again.

I hope your spirits have remained up since I left, and I'm
quite sure once you see your grandchild you'll see how
wrong you were to be upset over its coming. Nothing can
compare to a grandmother's joy over the birth of the first: a
baby of your very own without the usual messy and
inconvenient ways of getting it. No news from Wollongong
on my return incidentally, but what did I expect? Lesley has
no idea I visited you. As far as she's concerned I could have
been lying here dead since the 20th ult.

I enclose a card for Karen for you to forward if necessary,
as I don't know where she'll be staying. I've sealed it, but
there is no big mystery – just a 'get well' and
'congratulations' combined.

Remember what I said about Christmas, and start
looking at the catalogues. If we go early and come back

early, we'll be back in plenty of time before Karen needs us
you. And forget Saga – I don't want to be stuck with a load
of old people.

With kindest regards, your friend,

Irene

P.S. I had forgotten to cancel the milk. Am sending some
cream cheese under separate cover. Hope first class post is
working!

4th July

My Dear Karen,

Just a little 'thank you' note for all our lovely chats. If I had a daughter like you I'd count myself as truly blessed – I can't think what your mother finds to complain about. Try to be kind to her dear; our generation had different ideas about things, and not all of us have managed to adapt our way of thinking as yet. I've thought over your little problem quite a bit, and I stick by what I said before – don't tell her till after it's born. You never know, it might be very pale, and she might never need to be any the wiser. I know for a fact she has racist tendencies, since she wrote to me recently about a 'foreign accent' in an unflattering way, so it's as well to keep your own counsel till she's had time to fall in love with it. In the meantime, I'll try to drop the odd casual mention about the plus side of our Commonwealth friends. Don't hesitate to ring me if you need a chat.

Fondest wishes,

'Rene'

10th July

Dear Irene,

Yesterday a large pot of cream cheese was delivered by parcel post. When I say 'delivered', I mean flung out of a post office vehicle cruising at approx. 75 m.p.h. down the wrong side of the road. Fortunately I wasn't standing on the doorstep, so escaped most of the resulting explosion. The hydrangea took the full force of the blast and I was half an hour with the hosepipe ridding it of a substance reminiscent of the droppings of an incontinent pterodactyl (did I mention we were on to dinosaurs in my Natural History lectures?). It wasn't until I got your letter this morning – six days by first class post – that I realised what a kind thought had gone astray. I'm sure it would have been delicious. As it was, I had to give my hair three washes and my gardening gloves are fit for the dustbin.

Karen is much better thank you. I passed on your card. I think you do right to seal everything, given the current state of the post office, though I did think sticky tape *and* sealing wax was going a bit far. I'm sure she was pleased, though she hasn't mentioned. Too busy wondering whether sheep's yoghurt has Listerine in it. She says she won't touch anything that could harm the 'unborn foetus'. I ask you, what a way to talk about your first baby! I said to her, if you worried about everything you ate, you'd end up starving. She said she supposed I wanted her to go polluting the 'unborn foetus' with meat force-fed on excrement. I don't know where she gets her lavatorial expressions. Though, come to think of it, Gerald did keep a secret diary ...

She's got a library of books on child care – I pointed out she is only eight weeks pregnant – and says she is bringing the baby up 'green'. I said that would certainly be preferable to black, but she gave me such a funny look I had to explain I was joking.

I keep turning over and over in my mind where I've gone wrong with Karen. My own father threatened to horsewhip me if I ever brought home 'trouble'. He was a powerful man but had a wonderful sense of humour. The vicar's sermon this week was all about how dead friends and relations can see us and what we're doing. My father must be turning in his grave – thank God he was short-sighted. I mentioned it to Karen, but she told me not to be 'mawkish'. Thank Heavens for Howard! At least I have one child I can be proud of. I enclose a note from Karen which has just arrived. I must remember to pass on your address, and will close now as I think I have a migraine coming on. I've been too depressed to go to the travel agent.

Yours,

Vera

P.S. *You've* obviously cheered up if you can banter words with the bus conductor. I've tried chatting to mine – mostly about the state of the bus service – but he's a surly brute.

P.P.S. What 'militant' talks did you have with Karen?

8th July

Dear Rene,

Thanks for the advice – much appreciated. Haven't said a word to mum – you know what she's like. Will ring soon. Can't visit anyone at the mo' due to morning sickness.

Cheers,

Karen

24th July

My dear Vera,

Just a brief note to see if you've received the Caribbean holiday brochures I sent you. I've tried phoning but only get that continuous tone that usually denotes an unpaid bill! I am very busy organising a Bring and Buy and a non-stop 48-hour KeepFitathon at the church hall against the proposed siting of a nuclear dump under the golf links at Grossthorpe. Feelings are running very high here in Hethergreen and surrounding districts, and everybody is pulling their weight, including the cricket team, who are all keen golfers to a man, and who are doing a sponsored pub crawl. Arthur's just been round for his sponsorship, and was very insistent that I gave him your address. Hope you don't mind. Must fly as Bruce and I are having a breakfast meeting this morning to discuss strategy over the Tombola. Post card from Lesley yesterday saying that they love it over there. Typical.

Fondest regards

Irene

28th July

Dear Irene,

You are right to keep yourself busy, it's the best cure for desperation. I have scoured the house from top to bottom and finally tackled Gerald's cupboard, which I haven't been able to touch since he died. It took me an hour to prize off the padlock and then I wished I had let well alone. I found some things of a deeply distressing nature, of which I will only say that I now see where Karen gets her depraved behaviour. Howard, thank God, has always favoured my side. He is such a dear. His invitation to visit the Derby Dales came just in the nick of time and I am off there for the weekend. I shall take the brochures to pore over at leisure. I've opened a couple, but somehow all those pineapples just make me feel bilious.

Have a couple for me on your pub crawl,

All the best,

Vera

P.S. My phone has been off the hook as I have been getting 'nuisance' calls.

30th July

My poor dear Vera,

I am writing post haste to simply say 'confide in me'. I had a similar experience over Clive's last effects. Write to me and tell me everything. Any chance of letting me have the less offensive artefacts for my Bring and Buy?

All my warmest wishes and sympathy,

Irene

Irene Spencer

34 Wormwold Way

Hethergreen

Dear Irene

Howard has assured me that what I found was no more than George's Masonic Regalia.

The Derby Dales are wonderfully refreshing, as you can see from this picture. Majestic vistas and quite delightful dwellings. Howard and Antony live in a converted sheep bothy. They are turning it into an Alternative Health and Therapy centre and I must say I've never known there were so many different cures! I am writing this from the pub, next door where I'm downing a pint of "Shepherds ruin".

Feeling much more cheerful,

Yours as ever,

Vera

'Rainstorm Over Shap', photo by Scott Godber.

19th August

Dear Vera,

What a hectic and happy few days I've had having Karen here! Shopping became a joy again. She's such a lovely girl, I really can't imagine why the two of you don't click better. I hope you've got over having the hump with us now – I had no idea she was planning to visit, and I don't think *she* did till she was half way up the motorway. It just so happened that she was giving me a foot massage when you rang, so naturally it was all a bit giggly. I don't know where you get your conspiracy ideas from – Karen said you've been watching too much 'Dynasty'!

I'm really writing to find out your views on the Caribbean hols. If we don't book soon we'll be bitterly disappointed and end up going somewhere we don't like with no bathroom facilities. Karen says that St Kitts is particularly nice, or so a friend told her. It certainly looks ravishingly pleasant in the brochure (page 31 – I particularly like the look of Harry's Hideaway – what about those bananas!)

I was pleased to hear in your last that Gerald's worst fault was being a Mason. One day if I get really tiddly, I'll tell you what I found out about Clive whilst sifting through his effects. You think you know somebody after forty years of marriage, only to find you'd been in utter ignorance. When I think back over how blind and naive I was – but I'm just playing into the hands of my hypertension. Karen told me that when I feel myself getting het up, I should change the subject and dwell on something pleasant.

I hope you don't mind, but she confided in me about Howard. I must admit I had started to wonder. I think you're marvellous, accepting it so naturally. I talked it over with Bruce from a religious point of view, but he was very non-committal. According to him you can argue it both ways, depending on which biblical texts you choose as your reference. But I suppose when you're looking to have your own parish in the near future, you have to be very circumspect about controversy.

It seems strange to me that you can forgive Howard for the way he is, but can't seem to come to grips with Karen. I mean, any girl can make one mistake and 'catch her toe', but Howard must be sinning on a nightly basis. Is it because he's your son do you think? I've always been very grateful for not having had a boy – I know I would have spoiled him to death. I suppose that most boys in Howard's predicament have had a very emotional relationship with their mothers.

Arthur Snushall has just nipped in to collect his sponsor money. It cost me half a week's pension – they managed to crawl round eighty-three pubs! He wanted to tell me about about it, but I cut him off. He can be a bore sometimes, even though he'd do anything for you. You obviously made a big impact on him at the Ladies Night. He was most insistent that I send you his warmest regards, and wonders when you'll be coming to stay again. Of course you know, I'm sure, that he's very happily married.

The house feels very empty without Karen, and I'm starting to have wanderlust again. If you're still feeling bilious I could come and look after you for a few days if you like. I could manage next week or the week after, but not the week after that, as that is when they are sending the bulldozers in and we're having a sit-in on the eighteenth tee. I don't know *what* I'll wear.

Hurry up and decide about our hols!

Warmest regards

Irene

25th August

Dear Irene,

I got stuck in the automatic bus doors on Friday and was cursed by the driver in fluent Caribbean. I've quite gone off it for a holiday – I'm not at all sure it's the right kind of 'colourful'. Perhaps you should take Karen as you seem to get on so well with her. She would jump at the chance of a free ride – she's always known a soft touch when she saw one. You could continue your confidence in Harry's Hideaway, where I'm sure the bananas would come in useful. Frankly, one look at them would turn a Sumo wrestler bilious.

As for your obscure remarks about Howard, they are both puzzling and hurtful. I've always known Karen was deeply jealous of her brother (it started when they were children – he was sensitive and clever, as well as better looking) but I had no idea she went round fabricating stories about his 'relationship' with me. What on earth is she suggesting? Personally, I can't see a thing wrong with 'the way he is'. Vegetarianism is becoming all the vogue. This week I've done several wonderful things with a Cauli, and if you consider a few pints of 'local brew' after a hard day's Colonic Irrigation 'sinning', then you are even more narrow-minded than I thought. Perhaps Bruce isn't the only one who's thinking to have his own parish?

I'm afraid it's not convenient for you to visit at the moment, as I've invited Audrey Roscoe. She's such good company, always up for a gossip and a giggle. I must tell you what she said about Clive sometime. Good luck with the sit-in. I should wear that bathing costume you 'impulse' bought last summer. Should be enough to frighten a bulldozer.

Yours,

Vera

P.S. I've discovered it is Arthur Snushall who's been making the 'nuisance' calls. If his wife thinks she's happily married, I can only say 'poor creature'.

The Manse
The Green
Hethergreen

6th October

Dear Mrs Small,

I wonder if you remember meeting me at the luncheon table of our mutual friend, Mrs Irene Spencer? I found your address in her book and take the liberty of writing, which intrusion I hope you will forgive in the circumstances.

You may be aware that we in Hethergreen and surrounding parishes mounted a demonstration against the building of a nuclear waste dumping site under the golf links at Grossthorpe a few weeks ago, but you may not have read in the newspapers of the consequences of this peaceful protest on our part. I enclose a cutting from the *Micklechester Mercury*. The lady in question was our mutual friend.

Irene came out of her coma early last week and most of the injuries (fortunately bruises and grazes) are nearly completely healed. However, she is suffering from almost total amnesia, and since she is to be returned to the community soon, I am wondering if you might help. I know that she regards you as her closest friend – in fact, her first (and only) words on regaining consciousness were, 'You told me it'd frighten the bulldozer, Vera!' – perhaps you know what she meant? Since then she has become a deaf mute.

The doctors at the Micklechester Royal Infirmary feel that if her old friends were to remind her, as it were, of themselves and their common experiences, then her memory and her ability to communicate may be restored. Personally I am hardly surprised that her experiences have rendered her speechless. I have telephoned her daughter in

66

Australia, but unfortunately she is unable to come over at
the moment, due to an important Beach Barbecue she had
been planning for her husband's birthday.

Could you find time to jot her a few lines about yourself
– and indeed, herself? If you cast your mind about, I am
sure you can find many suitable memories – even if it were
only to talk about the war, which inevitably made a great
impression on people of your generation. My own
acquaintance with her is unfortunately too short to have
made much impression on her consciousness, and when she
does seem to recognise me at all, she appears to mouth
'Clive'. Would you know who that might be?

It seems she kept herself rather to herself in the parish,
and whereas she is not exactly without friends, there is
nobody locally who knows her intimately. I do hope you
may be able to help, as I am soon to take up my duties in my
new parish of Cynnington some hundred miles away, and it
would be a comfort to know that a good friend was taking
responsibility for her recovery.

God bless and keep you,

Yours

Bruce

REV. BRUCE SPRINGTHORPE

SEX-MAD GRANNY NUKES BULLDOZER

DRUG-crazed hippies went on the rampage at Grossthorpe Golf Club yesterday, damaging a bulldozer and turning the green grass of the eighteenth tee into blood-soaked furrows.

Greenkeeper Jack Maythorpe wept as he described the carnage. "It'll be six months before anybody can play a ball on that surface," he said, as he was led away by grieving relations.

The unprovoked mayhem started at 10.00 a.m. when CEGB workmen went peacefully about their business of building a much needed dumping site for spent fuel rods underneath the Grossthorpe Links.

CEGB had planned to remove and replace the turf and topsoil after burying the waste, thereby preserving the ecological balance — a dream now shattered by the ruthless damage done to the green by the hundreds of NIMBY (Not In My Back Yard) hippies' unsuitable footwear ripping it to shreds.

Further damage was done when a sex-mad granny (83), as yet unnamed, wearing only a multi-coloured lurex bathing costume and high heels, maliciously headbutted a bulldozer driven by Mr Ken Haggard.

"She came at me like a screaming fury," said Mr Haggard, who is now being treated for shock at Mickle-chester Royal, "waving her arms in a threatening manner. I had been ordered to pursue my duties and it was more than my job was worth to down tools." Allegations by the hippies that the ageing beauty queen had been trying to warn Mr Haggard of a small child in his path have proved groundless.

Inspector Gravers of Micklechester CID, in charge of the investigation, is waiting for her to help the police with their enquiries. "At the moment she is suffering from psychosomatic unconsciousness which is all in her head," said the Inspector, a keen student of psychology in his spare time, "which in my experience is a sure sign of a psychopathic mind unable to come to terms with their own guilt after an act of violence."

Turn to page 35 for results and reports on the Netherthorpe Amateur Golfing Championships.

9th October

Dear Rev. Springsteen,

I was horrified by your letter. It was I who advised Irene to meet trouble head on – needless to say, I never expected her to take me quite so literally. I will write to her straight away, through our 'shared past' is limited to a couple of years. I've no idea what she was doing in the war, though she did mutter darkly once about her war being 'wasted'.

Of course I remember meeting you. We talked about the gay priesthood and Cliff Richard and you told me you were setting the 23rd psalm to rock music. Good luck in your new billet – I hope they appreciate flair. I still remember the shocking pink shirt under the dog collar! Irene will miss you dreadfully, of course. That is, she would if she knew who you were. Clive is her deceased husband and I've always had the impression she doesn't miss him at all. Perhaps, in her troubled mind she is returning to the early days of their courtship when she sees you. You know, I am sure, that she had a soft spot for you. It must be a bitter blow for you too, to leave her, especially in such a state, but 'The Lord Giveth and The Lord Taketh Away', as she once said to me when I mislaid my dentures.

God bless you too,

Yours faithfully,

Vera Small

9th October

My Dearest Irene, (you do remember your name, I hope!)

I'm so sorry to hear of your plight. It's one thing having the odd lapse (I frequently forgot who Gerald was when I had to introduce him) but quite another living in a total void. I've enclosed a few things that might jog your brain waves. The photograph of us was taken at Lesley's (your daughter's) wedding – I'm the one with the sherry trifle in my hand. The other artefacts might put you in mind of Clive, though Gerald was a larger man altogether.

Now … where to start? Perhaps at the beginning (as you are, as it were, a clean sheet to be written on!). I was 17 when war broke out. I was in the hen-house at the bottom of our yard, looking for Clara who'd gone very broody, and I'd just bent over to see if she was hiding behind the hutch when I felt a sharp pinch on my bottom and a loud voice said, 'Better keep that well covered now the Hun is coming'. Well of course it was our next-door neighbour, Ray Hatchett who was a devil for catching you unawares. I had to be very careful when I was hanging out the washing. I must have gone the colour of my jumper (Schiaparelli shocking, as it came to be known later) because he said, 'Now, now, girl, this is no time to have a stroke, we've just declared war on Hitler'. I dropped everything and ran straight into the house to make sure my mother was alright. She was sitting with her ear glued to the radio and gravy was dripping down the wall from where my father had just flung his dinner. Silly isn't it, the things you remember?

I saw my boyfriend, Charlie, that evening. He was wondering if his hammer toe would delay his call-up papers. We danced until dawn at the tennis club (that is, I did – Charlie couldn't because of his hammer toe) and all the girls were crying. That Monday I gave in my notice at the milliner's where I'd been training and declared myself free for war work. Well my dear, that's enough for now. I don't want to tire you. Write as soon as you remember how to hold a pen and meanwhile here's a couple of 'teasers' for you ...

Caribbean holidays.

Karen's baby.

All the very best for a swift recovery,

Love,

Vera Small

20th October

Dear Mrs Small,

Thank you for your kind letter, which the hospital forwarded to me today. It must have arrived on the day I left, and then got snarled up in the system somewhere. There was quite a lot of blood on the envelope, which makes me wonder if it went to Casualty.

I stumbled on some other letters of yours the other day and I was wondering if you'd crop up again, since we have obviously shared some turbulent times. It looks from the last letter you wrote me before the accident as if I'd upset you in some way, for which I can only apologise and assure you that as far as I'm concerned, the 'hatchet' is well and truly buried. Clive was my husband – I know that from the irrefutable evidence I've found around the house, particularly a wedding photo – but then, I've also found another wedding photo where I appear to be getting married, so perhaps I was a bigamist? You say in that letter that a lady called Audrey Roscoe told you some amusing stories about Clive – could you share them with me, in case it strikes a chord?

I have got to grips with the fact that I have a daughter called Lesley, as she has phoned me a couple of times in the middle of the night. I can't say I'm much drawn to her, which is a dreadful thing for a mother to say, but she has a very shrill edge to her voice and seems to think I am to blame for everything that's ever happened to her. Bruce, a very nice vicar who seems to be a bit light on his feet and has been taking care of me, has obviously asked her, like you, to refresh my memory over certain incidents, and honestly, if I've been as wicked to her as she tries to make

out, it's a wonder the NSPCC didn't send me to the gallows
years ago. Apparently, she moved to Australia so
she wouldn't have to see me, but on the strength of
her nocturnal accusations, all I can say is 'good
riddance'.

I see from the newspapers that I used to be 'sex-mad',
but I can't say I've had many stirrings since. My solicitor
says that if it's not back in a couple of weeks, we must sue
for loss of sex drive, but I don't know if it's worth the fuss.
Apparently I'm in enough trouble already without
aggravating the police. I'm to be charged with obstructing
the CEGB in the pursuit of their duties, and wilful damage
to a bulldozer, which all sounds a bit far-fetched to me. But
then, every time I pick up a paper or turn on the television,
things seem to be far-fetched. Are we supposed to believe
the things they say in Parliament when they say it, or wait
until the next day when they say they didn't say it, in fact
they'd said the opposite?

It was interesting to read your reminiscences about the
war, and it reminded me that the day war broke out I started
my periods, which seemed to me to be much more
important at the time. My best friend Dolly had started hers
when she was twelve, and I at thirteen thought womanhood
would never come to me. As you say, the things you
remember!

Thank you for the brain teasers. Caribbean holidays is
easy, as it was in your last letter that you didn't want to go
any more due to a misunderstanding with a black bus
driver. Obviously we'd been planning to go. Karen's baby is
harder, but I think I've got to the bottom of it. It was a film
where everybody was pleased when she got pregnant, but
when it was born they realised it was the devil. Am
I close?

I hope you write to me again soon. Everybody round here
seems a bit embarrassed that I don't know them, but you

seem much more fun. I hope the second time around, you choose me for your friend again. Can I call you Vera in my next?

With love and gratitude,

Irene Spencer

30th October

My dear Irene,

I was very touched by your last. Of course you can call me Vera. In fact, I used to be known to my intimates as 'Vee' – all the girls at the dockyard had nicknames. Talking to you about the war has set off a lot of reminiscences. I even got an old photograph album out of the attic and had a flick through. I did laugh. Those trousers! We all seemed so happy, you wouldn't have thought there was a war on. I couldn't put a name to all of the faces, but I did remember Gerald (my husband) who was jolly good-looking in uniform, but terribly wet at kissing. Which brings me to your point about sex-drive. I never knew I had one until Gerald died, but looking at those pictures brought it all back to me. I felt a most peculiar stirring (I hope you don't mind my getting personal ... it might be useful for your solicitor); it was something like a hot flush, but pleasanter. In fact, I had to have a cold shower. It was the window cleaner's day and I didn't want him to arrive and find me all of a dither.

I got quite angry thinking about all we'd missed. When I look at Karen ...! (Karen's baby, by the way, will be my first grandchild and as far as I know, she hasn't been dabbling in black magic). In our day girls had to behave 'properly'. My father would have hit the roof, or rather his dinner would, if he'd found out I was 'going' with anyone. Between you and me, that didn't entirely stop me. I read *Forever Amber* when I was fourteen and there were one or two very steamy scenes on our annual chapel picnics. I particularly remember rolling in bluebells with Cecil who became a dentist. Of course, the girls at the dockyard were devils at egging each other on. We gave our boss a very hard time, always grabbing handfuls of him. You see they weren't types I'd have met in civvy street ... some of them were quite common. I got a graphic introduction to sex from Greta, one day when I was sent on an errand to the boiler room. There she was in a cloud of steam, with Bob Biggin going at it like a road drill. Of course he was a power tool operator.

You see, I was rather sheltered from 'life', apart from the cats and the chickens. My mother was a very reserved woman and never mentioned anything 'personal'. The day *my* periods started, I was too frightened to tell her. I stuffed a wad of newspaper from the lav down my knickers and ran down the road to my schoolfriend Jeannie, who gave me an aspirin and the 'doings'. Till the day she died my mother never knew I menstruated. Heaven knows where she thought I got Karen and Howard! I sometimes wonder that myself. Not Howard, of course, he's a darling, but I do so wish he'd settle down and have children. Trust it to be Karen who's producing!

What a shame Lesley has taken that attitude. I don't know. You worry yourself sick over daughters and they only throw it back in your face. I remember sitting up all night to make Karen a lovely little frock for a party. She went to it wearing black tights, a black skirt and Gerald's long black sweater. She looked like the bride of Dracula. Of course, if I said anything, her lip would curl and she would spit, 'I can't go round like Little Bo-Peep – times have changed mother'. Yes indeed, times have changed – but people haven't, as I would frequently tell her. Divorced, pregnant and abandoned by her lover, she's found out that one the hard way.

Well my dear, all for now. I hope you're eating plenty of fish. Let me know if you'd like a visit.

Yours very affectionately,

Vera

P.S. What's all this about being a bigamist?

P.P.S. I think we'll leave Audrey's stories of Clive until you are feeling stronger.

4th November

Dear Vera,

Thank you for another lovely letter. When you said you used to be known as 'Vee', it struck a big chord, and I wonder if your maiden named used to be Day? I certainly remember very strongly feeling a great affection for a couple of people (have you a sister?) called V.E. Day and V.J. Day. I can't think why I didn't know them by their Christian names.

My recovery is going apace. I got my hearing back before leaving hospital, which I can't say has been much of a comfort, since the only people who have been speaking to me are that awful girl, Lesley; my solicitor, who keeps saying, 'That'll be another hundred pounds please', and the police, and the conversations have been rather one-sided. However, a few days ago when I was out shopping for a couple of chops for the barbecue (barbecues for one are fun – the dinner lasts longer, you feel it's an occasion, there's less washing up, and there's nobody to see the bits of charcoal round your mouth), a young man grabbed me by the collar, shoved a water pistol in my face, and said if I didn't give him my pension and my jewellery, I'd be dead. Before I knew what I was doing, I'd stamped on his instep, elbowed him in the solar plexus, and picking him up off the floor had hissed, 'Stealing from the elderly shrinks your goolies, you worthless haemorrhoid'. I don't know who was more surprised, him or me. I didn't dare make a citizen's arrest and march him to the police station in case they tried to get me on another assault charge, but I can tell you I was rather pleased with myself, and have been walking taller ever since. But imagine, those being my first words! I went straight back home and tried practising in front of the mirror, but so far all I can seem to manage are rude words, which is why I haven't phoned you – I'd hate you to get the wrong idea. I'm persevering, and so long as I have at least one swear word in the sentence, I seem to be able to manage. This morning I asked the milkman to leave half a pint of bastard cream! The strange thing is, I don't seem to care about the impression I make now, and in a way I'll be sorry if that wears off.

In the meantime, I've been fascinated by my apparent bigamy, and have been spending a lot of time staring at the two wedding photos, hoping it might jog my memory, but so far all I'm getting are impressions. There is the one of me with the man who was called Clive, and to be honest I'm not much drawn to him at all. He looks a self-satisfied bugger (heavens, I hope my foul mouth isn't going to get the better of my letter writing!), and from this vantage point I can't honestly think what I saw in him. I am not filled with love or tenderness when I look at him, more irritation and a vague memory of unacceptable bodily functions. But the other man! Well, I feel hot and cold, trembly knee-ed, that I'd do anything for him, anything. I hear his voice, I see him with his arm around me, holding me fast, saying in a strong clear voice, 'You and me, my darling, together, always, now and across the unknown aeons. Never leave me, for I should be lost entirely.' And I obviously did, and now he is. What can I have been thinking of? I feel very strongly that if only I could track him down I would know true happiness to the end of my days – but then again, I feel curiously contented now. Maybe I should have had a blow to the head years ago – I feel unconstrained, as if I've finally managed to get to the powder room and take off a crippling corset. Some days I wake up and think, I really should do that dusting, and then I think, sod that for a game of soldiers, and I go to the library instead, or go swimming. Last night I went to the pictures on my own and had a bag of popcorn and a hot dog and thoroughly enjoyed myself. The girl looked at me a bit askance when I gave her my two pounds and asked for one to see 'Rain Bollocks', but what do I care? If that boy Dustin Hoffman can get work with his appalling disabilities, then I can certainly pay my way to watch him at it.

If you feel like taking a real risk, I'd quite fancy an outing with you in the not-too-distant. What do you say – shall we go and paint the town red – or blue in my case? Could you cope? Write and let me know soon. I've got to go now as there's a man at the door wanting to read the frigging meter.

Lots of love,

Irene

7th November

My very dear Irene,

I've been casting around in my mind for an occasion it
might be appropriate to take you to with your current
affliction. The W.I. Autumn Fayre hardly seems it, I don't
think our chairwoman would take kindly to abusive
name-calling (though goodness knows I've often been
tempted), nor does the vicarage Bonfire Party appeal,
though the vicar, of course, is quite used to it.

I think I might have hit upon the solution, though. Our
local Am-Dram society is about to give their seasonal treat
at the Astor Arts and Crafts Centre, so how about coming to
that? So much language flies about between these theatrical
types, that if you called one of them a 'silly old bugger' to
their face, I doubt they would even notice. They are a gay
crowd and their first nights are notoriously pleasant.
Everyone gets squiffy in the bar before and after (and on one
occasion, during, if King Lear's hiccups were anything to go
by) and there's always a party at one or other of their
houses. To be honest, I've never been, though I've once or
twice been invited.

Gerald couldn't abide that crowd, which he always
referred to as 'the suede shoe brigade'. The only time I
managed to get him to a show (that thing about two tramps
– very boring) he fell asleep and snored loudly. Was my face
red! Gordon Scarth, the president of our Antiques and
Collectables Club, had 'directed' it and he was sitting right
next to me. I plied him with gin and tonics later and blamed
it all on Gerald's hayfever. Speaking of which, that is the
name of the piece the Astor players are giving. I believe it's
very light – not at all 'arty' – so I don't think it will tax
what's left of your poor old grey matter. It opens on the
Thursday, so why not come that afternoon and stay for the

81

rest of the weekend? I'll think of some other place we can visit without giving offence. I can't wait to try you on the 49 bus driver – do you know any Caribbean obscenities?

This business about a blow to the head is very intriguing. *I* was hit by a flying brick during an air-raid. I was concussed for a week and afterwards married Gerald. Now you've started me wondering …

Till next week, my dear,

With all love,

Vera

Grossthorpe Police Cells
18th November

Dear Vera,

As you can see from the above address, I am in dire
straits and beg you to help. When I got off the train at
Grossthorpe coming back from you, I went to get my car
from the station car park and bumped into Bruce, who was
about to get his train to Cynnington to take up his new
duties. A few parishioners were with him to see him off –
Beryl Mainwaring, who you met at the Ladies Night, Judith
Brain, and Marjorie Bostock. After we'd put him on the
train and waved it out of sight, we decided to go and have a
coffee in Grey's Coffee Lounge, but as we were walking
down the High Street, Veronica St John spotted us and
came over for a chat. All these girls, except Judith, had been
on the demonstration, and they were asking me how I was
and how I'd felt about being charged. We were all filling
Judith in and getting quite heated, and the next thing I
know, I'm being bundled into a police car, charged under
the Public Order Act. Apparently you aren't allowed to talk
to more than one person at a time in the street these days,
otherwise it's a political meeting or you're inciting them to
riot or something. Of course, my swearing affliction didn't
help – the girls found it quite amusing, and were copying
me, so I suppose we were getting a bit out of hand – and you
can imagine my surprised response to the two young
officers who arrested me. Or rather, I hope you can't, as I
believe I surpassed myself this time. My solicitor has read it
to me, blushing crimson all the time, as they had written it
all down in their notebooks to use as evidence against me.

This morning I was remanded in custody awaiting trial,
which could be for anything up to two years apparently,
owing to the queues. I am beside myself about Sidney. He's

83

already been in kennels for ages while I was in hospital, and I'd put him in again at the weekend when I was visiting you. I'm sure he'll pine and die before I get out. Would you, could you, please get him for me and look after him until my return? I know it's a big favour to ask – indeed, if things go against me, it could be a lifetime's job – but you are the only person I have ever seen him register affection with beside myself. He even used to go for Clive, and for a Giant Poodle, that's quite rare. He is at Pampered Pets Holiday Homes, Little Throssle 634. Forgive me for asking, but it's just one thing too many for me to worry about at the moment.

Apart from all this, I had a thoroughly enjoyable weekend with you, notwithstanding the drama at the play. I'm so sorry my memory had to return all in a rush like that during the quiet scene in the second act, but as I already explained to you, it was seeing that girl 'dry up' and hearing her 'prompt' called from the wings that sped me back in time to my first 'marriage'. It's nice to know I'm not a bigamist, but sad to think that he who I had come to think of as the great love of my life had only been Cyril Organ acting out his part in the title role of 'The Errant Spouse'. I hope you weren't too embarrassed afterwards. I must say, they were very decent about it in the bar.

Conditions here aren't too bad, except that they're too overcrowded to allow visits at the moment. I am sharing my cell with two very nice girls and their mother, who are all charged with murdering a rapist while in the course of his duties. How the other half live! My spirits have risen since a kind WPC showed me yesterday's *Mercury* – Marjorie Bostock and the girls are organising an 'Irene Spencer Is Innocent' Bring and Buy to try to raise my bail. I hope it's a good turn-out, as it's been set at a quarter of a million pounds.

Please write when you can. My solicitor is going to

84

smuggle this out for me and post it on to you, as apparently the censoring is awful. Yesterday, my cell mates received a letter, 'Dear Aunty Doris and Girls, ▅▅▅▅▅ ▅▅▅▅▅▅▅▅ ▅▅▅▅▅▅ ▅▅▅▅ ▅▅▅▅▅▅ ▅▅▅ ▅▅▅▅ ▅▅▅▅▅ ▅▅▅▅ ▅▅▅▅▅ All the best, Tracie Louise'.

Hope you are keeping well. Sorry to be a bother.

Lots of love,

Irene

P.S. Sidney hates tinned food of any kind except for salmon.
P.P.S. Irene Spencer is innocent!

26th ███████

My ███████ Irene,

This is ███████████! What ████████s those ███████████s must have been to ███████████ you, even if you did call them ███████ing ███████ ████ ██████████s (your solicitor rang me). I'm beginning to believe what Karen says about them; before I'd always put it down to ██████-wing paranoia? As for this ████████ing business, we shall just have to talk in code like ██████████s of war, shan't we?

Don't worry about Sidney, I've collected him and I must say he *was* glad to see me. I didn't have any salmon handy, so I gave him a tin of snails Howard bought on his last duty-free trip and, do you know, he wolfed them! I think my arms have grown a foot since we've been going 'walkies'.

I've been in touch with ███████████ about the ████████ and ███████ ██████████ and I'm mustering everyone able from here. The Great Potterton Players have really entered into the spirit and are going to mount a special show. I think it's 'Oh Calcutta'.

One word of advice – be careful who you fall in with there. Karen was taken to ███████████ once after a demo and the things she saw – unnatural acts using ██████████s and ██████████s, and that was only the warders!

Must go, Sidney is barking.

All my ████████,

Vera

Cell 4
Grossthorpe Police Station
4th December

Dear Vera,

Don't send your letters direct to the above address – I
could hardly decipher a word of your last, so full of blanks
was it. And anyway, I've heard on the grapevine that I'm to
be moved soon, I'm not sure where. Write c/o my solicitors,
Crabbe, Sidebottom and Partners, 5 Dresden St,
Grossthorpe, and Mr Ricketts will smuggle it to me,
wherever I am. Apparently he is going to give my briefs to a
lady barrister, which is what I call progress! He says she is
the best I can afford, as she is young and black and only a
woman, but I think he's jealous that he never got to wear a
wig and gown himself. (That looks rather queer written
down, doesn't it?)

The days go slowly in here, and even though I can't quite
get the meaning of your missive, I read it every night and
sleep with it under my pillow. Another girl joined us in our
cell yesterday, so now we are five. I must say she paints a
very attractive picture of prison proper, and I shall almost
be disappointed if I don't get 'sent down' (excuse my
criminal jargon). She defaulted on her mortgage payments,
got 'banged up' for four years, and came out with a degree
in Economics. Now she's got into trouble with her credit
cards, on purpose, so she can gain her PhD. She couldn't
get a grant for it on the outside.

The kind WPC came into the cell last night just before
lights out, removed her tunic, unbuttoned her shirt, and
stuck her chest out at me. Underneath she was wearing a
FREE IRENE SPENCER T-shirt. Judith Brain's husband
got his students to print them at the Polytechnic where he
works. I feel quite a celebrity! Brenda (the WPC) tells me

they're selling like hot cakes, which is good, as the proceeds are to go towards my trial costs (I think they've abandoned trying to raise the quarter of a million for my bail), but that she herself had been given hers by a working girl as a bribe for not 'running her in'. These are certainly treacherous times we are living in, if even a typist has to bribe the police not to arrest her.

Anyway, must sign off now as I've used up all this paper – sorry about the Bronco, but they're very stingy here with the stationery. It'll be Christmas soon, and I won't be able to send any cards. But then again, it'll be nice to have company. I *wish* you could visit me. Brace up Irene. No sniffles. *Non, je ne regret rien.*

Fondest love,

Prisoner F5138

P.S. Thank you so much for rescuing Sidney – you are a friend indeed. I hope he is 'behaving' himself, and that your arms will soon adjust to his strength. Give him a kiss and tell him Mummy loves him.

H.M. Prison at ▓▓▓▓▓▓▓▓▓

12th December

My dear Irene,

I've always wanted to visit one of Her Majesty's residences but would have preferred it to have been Buckingham Palace. This sojourn has nothing to do with voluntary work, nor indeed voluntary anything, and the food is abominable. I can only hope the Queen's personal cooks are of a more regal standard. Two days after I sent off your last letter Customs and Excise dropped in. Through the skylight. Others entered by the more regular route of the front door, but as this was locked and bolted at the time (4.15 a.m.) they left rather a large hole, having axed down three of the panels. Really, lager louts cause less damage!

Apparently they suspect me of being an International Drug Runner, but this I only learned after they had smashed my entire collection of Port Merion teapots and ripped up all the upholstery. I was 'gobsmacked', to use one of Karen's favourite phrases, quite literally, as I had a tea towel shoved in my mouth, I suppose to stop me screaming. When I'd recovered enough to speak, they demanded to know 'who or what was 'Sidney''. I should have thought that was self-evident as the poor lamb was shut in the kitchen, howling more ear-shatteringly than the Hound of the Baskervilles, but they persisted in thinking he was a euphonism for drug abuse, as is 'going walkies'. 'Salmon' is 'crack', 'snails' a type of psychedelic substance which makes you feel like a giant. It's all because I made a reference to talking in code in your letter. Speaking of which, I shall think twice next time I hear my Irish librarian say she had 'great crack' at the weekend!

This is being smuggled out for me by a charming Jamaican girl with whom I've been sharing a cell. She's going 'on parole' today, and thinks she may stay out long enough to post a letter. I haven't been allowed to see a lawyer until I 'confess', but I have had a visit from Karen, who has taken Sidney though how she will manage I don't know. She is hugely pregnant with swollen ankles and the baby is still two months off. I asked her if twins run in her ex-paramour's family. She said shortly that she had no idea if he even *had* a family and the only sort of twins he'd mentioned were carburettors. Try as I might, I can't picture that relationship.

Well my dear, I must close as Maxine has her running shoes on and is eager to be off. I don't know how long they can hold me without a charge. Karen says about a year, she thinks, so who knows, you might be getting a visit from me sooner than expected!

Keep your pecker up.

Love,

Vee

P.S. Can't bear to think what they're going to serve up for Christmas dinner. But, look on the bright side, Irene, it's an easy way to diet!

Cell 214,

H.M. Prison Ship *Pride of Cleveland*

20th December

My dear Vee,

What a chapter of incidence and coincidence! I have just heard on the grapevine that you and I are in the same boat, so to speak. Maxine was picked up almost immediately for possession of an offensive weapon (her afro comb) and was very upset not to have had time to post your letter. Imagine her surprise when she found she was sharing a cell with me! I'd just read your letter, and she was telling me how you'd been keeping their spirits up with songs from the Blitz and your impressions of the warders, when we were bundled up with our few possessions and shipped out here. Something about clearing the on-shore cells to cope with the anticipated rush of arrests following the amendment to the blasphemy laws – have you heard the same rumour on your deck?

News of your famous impersonations have reached our ears down here on Deck F – you are awful, I bet the Governor never said anything *like* that! – and Maxine said, 'It's got to be Vera!', and our contact said yes, she believed that was the name. We'd been hoarding a wine gum for some special celebration, and the six of us in here were all of one mind, to toast Vera! We each had a nibble, and honestly felt quite intoxicated afterwards, but I imagine that was more due to High 'Spirits'!!

Listen my dear friend, rest assured that you won't be in for much longer. I have made a deposition to my lawyer – well at least, I will have when I'm allowed to send it – stating your innocence re your connection with a drugs ring. I've written it all down on Bronco, but so far I haven't been able to post it due to staff shortages – apparently they're all calling in sick at the moment as they want to spend Christmas with their families. Don't we all?! Well no, actually, in my case, although I'd give anything to be the one to mince Sidney's giblets for him on The Big Day.

Hope you can read this – isn't it amazing how small you can make your writing when you've only got the one sheet? Tomorrow I shall try to save two so we can have a really good chin-wag. I'm going to give this to Janice now who's on kitchen duties, so she can give it to the girl on your deck. It's very pleasant, this feeling of comradeship, isn't it? No wonder they go on about the Brotherhood of Man. Seems silly that it's taken prison to introduce me to the Sisterhood of Women.

Oh well, so much for waxing philosophical. All for now my dear. Keep your spirits up.

All love,

Irene X

24th December

Dearest Irene,

The rumour *we* heard was that the police were expecting a post-Xmas deluge of wife beaters, rampaging Champagne louts and down-and-outs back on the streets after stints as Father Christmas. I must say your version is much more interesting and explains why a warder told me to turn round three times and spit when I mentioned Mrs Thatcher. Has she been deified? Perhaps the pope has made an unscheduled ground-kissing visit to Chequers while we've been 'inside'? Karen will be pleased – she told me long ago the Monarchy should be abolished. Speaking of Karen, I had a (censored) note from her on Friday. ████████ is in the best of health, though his barks are annoying the neighbours.

I'm delighted news of my 'cabarets' is reaching 'F' Deck. It *is* amazing what prison brings out in you. Of course, I always knew I was a performer. When I was a toddler my father's favourite trick was to tell me to go to the door and 'fetch it'. I'd get down on all fours and crawl to him with the paper. I've had prisoners and warders alike in tucks with my snatches of 'Guys and Dolls'. We're a bit short of 'guys' of course, but you'd be surprised what you can do with Sellotape and brown paper! I've made some very supportive friends. I completely agree with you about the 'Sisterhood', but I can't believe this is what Karen means. She never has a good word for any of her friends and is always enraged at their writing. I wonder what she'd think if she could read our correspondence? Probably that, like ████████, we are 'barking'.

I believe tomorrow we may meet, as due to staff shortages we're all to be herded together for our turkey roll and Smash potatoes. We're to be allowed to watch the Queen's speech, before being given our Librium.

Well, my dear, all for now as I am hanging up my stocking (hand-knitted by a lady at 'Release') and joining my cell-mates in a few heart-warming carols. I will think of you as I sing. A very Merry Christmas, my friend, and may we be able to greet the New Year free in Spirit, if not in body.

Your own Vera

94

Solitary Cell C
Christmas Day

My dearest, dearest Vee,

How *good* it was to see you today, and to be lucky
enough to sit next to you during the Queen! Never has
human contact ever meant so much to me. Sitting there in
the dark, save for the flickering illumination of Her Majesty,
holding your hand – it's the best Christmas present I could
ever wish for. Forgive me for weeping so foolishly. It was
just that, being so near you, it put me in mind of all the
happy times we've shared on the 'outside' – and the
heartache. It's true what they say, isn't it – you don't know
what you've got till it's gone.

What a wonderful idea of yours to swap socks for our
Christmas presents to each other. Now all I need do when
I'm blue and missing you is to look at my feet! You are a
dear.

Please don't be upset about me being caught talking to
you. I honestly don't mind the thought of solitary now that
I've seen you, and it's only for five days. My greatest hope is
that I can behave myself well enough for them to honour
their promise and let me out in time for the so-called New
Year 'celebrations', so I might have the chance to see you
again. I have found a small hole round a pipe that runs
through this cell, and have ascertained that it goes right
through to the cell above, by whispering and knocking. A
nice woman called Susan, who is in for writing rude words
on her water shares application, says that she'll smuggle
this note to you if I push it up to her. Do you know her? She
sounded as if she knew you, but then, as we know, your
celebrity runs before you!

Vee, when we get out of here (note I don't say if!), shall
we set up house together? Being in here, despite the bad

things, I *have* enjoyed the company. I don't think I could bear to go back to my lonely house in Hethergreen after this, by myself. If we teamed up, we could sell one or both of our houses, pool our resources, and live the life of Riley. We could even have Karen and the baby to stay with us at first, if she has nowhere else to go. Only two months to go before the birth of her first, and no mother to lean on – she must be going frantic.

What I was trying to tell you when I got caught is that I've had a letter from Lesley. It was so nasty, they'd left it completely uncensored – I suppose it's only the nice, supportive, friendly things they cut out, the devils. In it, she told me that word had spread to Woollongong about my 'evil deeds', and that after a 'family conference' with Keith, they have decided to cut me out of their will! As if that matters to me! It's true that since she's shown her true colours, I've often wished her dead, but not for any financial advantage to me. Anyway, that's as nothing to the rest. They have told my little Cheryl Marie that Nanna has gone to Heaven. How could they? Lesley says it is to save her from the stigma of having a convict for a relative, but I'd have thought that in Australia, *not* having one in the family would stigmatize you even more. Anyway, I'm not going to let it upset me – I've got enough on my hands – and if necessary I'll just have to wait until Cheryl Marie is old enough to open her own mail, before I can let her know the good news that I'm alive – and well.

You may be surprised at the length of this letter, but the one advantage of being in solitary is not having to share the Bronco! I could go on for a whole roll, but I must keep this thin enough to push through the hole to Susan.

The warder just came in to give me my night medication, so I'll have to sign off now as I can already feel myself nodding off. Happy Boxing Day, my dear. I shall think of you over the turkey goulash. I'm going to wear my socks in bed tonight, as a special holiday treat. They can't take *that* away from me! My feet in your socks, my hand in yours. What a day!

All love and seasons greetings,

Irene xx

December 29th

Dear Irene,

I was rather troubled when I received your last. Frankly
you sound unhinged in it. 'My feet in your socks, your hand
in mine'! What is this? Some kind of suicide love pact?! Do
be careful, my dear. Surrounded as we are by censoring eyes
and ears, you don't want to say things that give the wrong
impression! (Susan, by the way, works in the sewer block
with me. She's working class, though a well meaning soul.
She fancies herself as an artist and has done colourful
'primitives' on her cell wall. The Authorities won't provide
her with paints, so she's made use of bodily functions.)

Thank you for your lovely extra present – a paper-maché
toothmug is just what I've always wanted. Did you chew up
all that Bronco yourself? What a labour of love. I managed
to smuggle out a Christmas token to Howard (a crust of
bread with my teethmarks in it) and yesterday I was allowed
a visit from him. He brought me a belated Christmas gift (a
goatskin smock and half a pound of Muesli) and an
admission. He is 'gay'. He said I wasn't to worry, he and
Antony are thoroughly monogamous and they've both been
HIV tested. I said that reassuring as that was, it wouldn't
help with the neighbours. He said he was very sorry, he
knew I'd be upset, but he couldn't live a lie any longer, he
was sick of 'being in the closet'. The word 'closet' put me in
mind of that Masonic business of Gerald's I found. Again, I
can't help wondering ...

I can't deny it is a momentous shock, though, if I'm
honest, I knew there was 'something'. I blame my mother
who had knitted him pink. People were always stopping by
his pram to say 'who's a lovely girl then?' I cried all night at
the thought of my lost grandchildren. But today, my
cellmate Beefy (an Ex-Hell's Angel) has given me a

heart-to-heart on people of 'the other persuasion'.
Apparently they are not as I'd supposed, plain and
unattractive, but can be quite normal, just like us. They
have dogs and are kind to old people. I can't say I'm
completely reconciled, but Beefy has promised that if I
cheer up she'll do a tattoo on my navel.

Howard said that Karen's had a nasty bout of flu. The
hospital have told her she'll have to have a home birth as
they've got no beds. I do so wish I could be with her.

Vee

P.S. Only a couple of days to go before you are back among
us!

Cell 214

1st January

Dear Vera,

A pinch and a punch for the first day of the month, and quite frankly, a good kick in the behind for being so rude in your last. 'Unhinged'? You try being in solitary in the bowels of a ship with no heating in a force 8 gale, then let's talk about 'unhinged'! In those conditions you cling to the happy memories of warm friendship, or what you had been led to believe was warm friendship, anyway. I suppose you'll be accusing me of coming out of the cupboard next, or whatever you call it. As for Howard – how could you have been so blind? I tried to tell you once, but you refused to hear me. And so what, if they love each other? You're so prejudiced and narrow-minded sometimes, a thing that Karen has often pointed out to me that I am not. And I know another thing that you're going to have to swallow in the not-too-distant, so I just hope that your experiences in here will have made you more tolerant and a bit less anxious to condemn.

They let me out of solitary yesterday, so I was at the New Year's Eve celebration and saw you making a fool of yourself with who I can only assume is she who is known as 'Beefy'. Who *wants* a mermaid tattooed round their navel? You'll have to live with that for the rest of your life. Everybody in my cell thinks that you've gone stir-crazy. I didn't come over and say hello, as you seemed to be having a whale of a time without me. My mother always warned me about people who transfer their affections easily, but I have never learned. The girls in my cell say it is because of my low self-esteem, and they are trying to raise my conscience about it each day after slop-out.

My good news, if you're interested, is that the lady barrister has prepared my briefs and we are taking them before the Court quite soon. *They* won't tell me when, but they say I'll know when I am blindfolded in a dinghy, being rowed ashore. I just wish I was a better sailor – I feel queasy at the thought.

Not one to bear malice, I wish you a Happy New Year among your new friends.

With all good wishes for your future.

Irene

Prisoner 290001
Cell Block H

Wensdy

Deer Ireen,

Vee has arsked me to write this four her as she is indisposd dew to a nastee bowt of blood poisnin. I had simlar with my 'Satan livs' tattoo, but that was dun with a pin. She is verry sory you hav taken agenst her and wants to make it up beefour she dise? Diys? Dyes, which is onlee to likeley as I dun hers with a fork.

She sends orl her luv and hops yor breefs will be easy.

Yrs faithfullee

Beefy

P.S. Her dorter went into prematur laber last nite but hasunt had a result yet.

12th January

'Dear' Beefy,

At last I am free. Say goodbye to Vera for me. I am in the dinghy, afloat on the great sea of life, and apart from the biliousness, I feel very optimistic. My trial begins tomorrow. I shall win.

It is such a comfort to know that Vera is in your hands, and off mine. She is such a responsibility and has quite a vicious temper. Furthermore she is selfish, egotistical, vain, and not a fit mother. I shall be taking care of Karen and her baby on my release, as that is what she wants. It will be better if Vera stays away from us, as we shall have our hands full of nappies, and will be able to do without having to minister to the needs of her second childhood. The baby's father is a West Indian, by the way. Break the news to Vera as brutally as you like.

All good wishes for a wonderful life in prison together.

Yours,

Irene Spencer,
An innocent and soon-to-be free woman.

H.M. Prison Ship *Pride of Cleveland*

21st April

Dear Mrs Spencer,

I am so very pleased your trial has gone smoothly and your days of captivity are over. Careful not to fall behind with the Poll tax, or we shall be seeing you back again. Ha! Ha! Yes, everyone here gave a very big cheer when they heard of your acquittal on the grounds of diminished responsibility. Everyone, that is, except poor Vera Small, who has passed into what appears to be a terminal coma and has not murmured a word since your last was read out to her. On removal to the hospital wing, she was thought to sigh 'Oh Irene . . .', but her friend Beefy insisted it was merely the air escaping from her catheter. Beefy has indeed been a devoted nurse, running herself ragged to fulfil all Vera's (unspoken) needs. Never have I witnessed so much energy expended for so little return; at this rate Beefy will shortly be hospitalised also. I don't know what denomination you follow, or indeed if your experiences here have rendered you totally Godless, but can I, as a man of faith, beg you to send one word of forgiveness? You may have had a serious falling-out with Vera, but I cannot believe you wish her dead, or at least, not without your blessing. Your solicitors tell me you are selling your house and moving away. I fervently pray this reaches you before you commit the irrevocable.

God bless,

Rev. Trev. (prison chaplain)

P.S. Vera has a granddaughter, as I expect you know. Her

daughter has made several attempts to bring her out of the coma by dangling the baby in front of her face. She explained to Beefy it was 'shock' therapy, but so far never a flicker.

The Vicarage,
Cynnington

27th April

Dear Trev,

How *are* you, you old son of a gun? I couldn't believe it
when Irene Spencer passed me your letter. I'd no idea you
were working on a prison ship these days. *Bonjour matelot*! I,
for my sins, have recently taken over the parish of St
Cuthbert the Untainted, and am having a whale of a time
judging marrows and eating seed cake. Come over and see
me some time when you get shore leave, and we'll finish
that debate about the Ascension that we never quite
resolved at the Varsity. Have you heard from Chris and
Jumbo recently? I had a postcard from them at Christmas –
they really are a scream.

I'm sorry to hear about Vera Smalls. Mrs Spencer, an
ex-parishoner of mine, is alarmed to hear of her imminent
death and has asked me to write, sending her blessing. At
the moment she has her hands pretty full as she is looking
after Vera's daughter Karen and her new-born baby, and is
organising a 'Vera Smalls Is Innocent' Fork and Finger
Buffet. She has asked me to ask you to ask Vera for the
recipe for the Blue Cheese Dip. You may have read in the
papers about her sensational trial, but if not, I enclose a
cutting. Read it to Vera and see if you get a flicker.
Apparently it's crucial that you do, as the Blue Cheese Dip
is central to the theme of the Buffet. Irene also suggests that
you shout 'Beef up Vera', very loudly in her left ear (she's a
bit Mutt and Jeff in her right).

Hope you can bring it off. Shall I buy you a ticket to the
bunfight? Irene's cooking is quite legendary. Tell Vera that
Howard will be there – he's her number one son, and a

great friend of mine. Irene and Karen are staying with him in the Derby Dales at the moment, so send the recipe care of him, Sheepdipper's Shed, Shooters Hill, Shale, Shap, Nr Great Shagthorne, Derbs. And write to me soon, you old reprobate!

Yours ever, in love and peace, sickness and health,

Bruce Springthorpe

The Daily Satellite, 12th April

SEX-MAD GRANNY IS LOCO, SAYS JUDGE

Hundreds of ex-prisoners, OAPs, ethnic minorities and peace loonies cheered in court yesterday when diminutive Irene Spencer was officially declared mad and set free.

In his address to the court at the end of the trial, Judge Branston Pickles said that her voluntary sterilisation had tipped the balance in her favour, and that he was returning her to the community 'for better or worse'.

Asked for her comments outside the Old Bailey, buxom Irene (85) read from a sheet of Bronco which she had prepared earlier, stating the innocence of her 'friend' Vera Smalls (96).

Vera, still serving time for drugs running, is currently in a coma on a prison ship off the British Isles and official sources say that she is 'very poorly'.

Close friends and relatives are preparing themselves for the worst, but Irene, who claims she is neither, is battling on to free her. "If they think I'm mad," says Irene, "they should meet Vera. She is completely barking, and should be released."

H.M. Prison Ship *Pride of Cleveland*
3rd May

Brucie baby!

How fabby dabby to hear from you. Chris and Jumbo told me you were dead. Something about a contaminated jab when you were out in the Tropics. They're so pleased to know it was a false alarm, or rather they will be in six months when they get my letter. They are currently up the Orinoco camping with Pongo and Gerry.

Well, well, you old rugger bugger, reading your letter brought it all back, great times eh? D'you still keep up with your sport? Hope all that cake isn't sending *you* to seed! I'm still rowing. As you can imagine, in my present billet it's nothing short of essential. I've got an arrangement with a jolly tar – we take it in turns in the dinghy! I'd love to come and see you. I get leave twice a year (more if I threaten to expose the horrors of ship board life ... I've got a nice one up my cassock about the governor and the stoker) so I'll pop along to the Fork and Finger. Meanwhile I enclose a missive from Vera Small who has made a miraculous recovery. I'd like to think it was the laying on of hands that did it, but Vera insists her friend Beefy had been doing that for weeks to no avail, so it must have been the cutting. Certainly, when I shouted 'Vera Small ... 96' in her left ear a strange seizure overcame her. She's now back to normal, or as normal as I gather she ever is – spends all day pacing her cell and ranting at poor Beefy who has lost a stone and was yesterday found dangling from a porthole.

Yours in Christ, till we meet again,

Your ever loving,

Trevor

TO WHOM IT MAY CONCERN

Vera Small wishes it to be known that she entirely disassociates herself from anything said or done by Irene Spencer in the so-called 'Vera Small Is Innocent' campaign. As for the blue cheese dip, the recipe is a family secret, though not one, you may be sure, that has been, or ever will be, passed on to her ungrateful children.

She would like to remind certain persons whom it is that stood collateral for the mortgage on Sheep Shagger's Bottom or whatever it's called and indeed who has paid the gas and electricity for the last two quarters, not to mention settling a bill for outstanding rent with her beggarly daughter's landlord. She is in touch with her solicitor about her will, so let them put that in their pipes and smoke it whilst thinking of her lying in this stinking hold. And no, I am not referring to the embraces of Beefy, whose personal hygiene has improved immensely since sharing a cell with a civilizing influence and whose affection is not, unlike that of some others, in question. She may be rough but she is always more than ready.

Vera is currently fully engaged in teaching Beefy to read and write and will shortly be starting her own campaign to bring literacy to Her Majesty's prisons. She is sure she will find joy in contributing to the wider good and thus recover from the terrible hurt done her by her family and 'friends', who cannot, it seems, be bothered to write her a letter!

Sheepdipper's Shed

8th May

Darling Mummy,

Bruce Springthorpe has just given us your To Whom It May Concern, and we're all terribly upset. How can you have got it so wrong? We all love you desperately, and are literally working night and day to get you out of that terrible place. I couldn't bear seeing you there at Christmas – I'm not ashamed to say that I wept for days afterwards. Irene has been an inspiration to us all, never giving up, battling on through thick and thin, always confident that Right will triumph. She has even made bold attempts to get Beefy released too so that you can be together when you get out, and honestly, I don't think there is a greater love than that.

Darling Mums, please let us help you. Irene knows what she's doing. You have to be mad to get out of prison these days, it's the only way. Please trust us and play along. We're having a big fund-raising party for you in a couple of days, and we're hoping to get lots of publicity. Nigel Norris of the *Shagthorne Gazette* has given a definite yes, but we're still working on Jimmy Young.

I wish you could be with us, Mummy. We all miss you and talk about you all the time. Come home to us. All you have to do is roll your eyes and slobber a bit – is that too much to ask?

Eat this when you've finished reading it. It's on organic brown rice paper which I've impregnated with Gentian Flower Remedy – it'll cheer you up.

```
XXXXXXXXXX              XXXXXXXXXX
 XXXXXXXX    All my love,  XXXXXXXX
  XXXXXX                   XXXXXX
   XXXX                     XXXX
    XX         Howie         XX
    X                        X
```

Sheepdipper's Shed

8th May

My dear Vera,

Please be nice and come out of prison. Poor darling Howard is going off his head, and the worry is undoing all the good work he did on himself in the Flotation Tank last year. I'm sorry that you think it's so dreadful that I love your son and that he loves me. Personally, I can't think of anything nicer. Except for both of us to have your love too.

This funny-looking note-paper is organically farmed seaweed which I've smeared with Royal Jelly – that's what the Queen takes, and look how marvellous she is. In fact, I know several old queens who do very well on it indeed! Oh dear, camp joke, whoopsee. Hope you've still got your sense of humour.

Oh well, I'd better drag myself up and get back in the kitchen – there's still acres of pastry to roll out for your party.

Till we meet again, lots of love ducks, and a big kiss.

Antony x

c/o Sheepdipper's Shed

8th May

Mum

For Christ's sake stop being pig-headed, grow up, and get your arse in gear. It's horrible here with everybody weeping and wailing all the time, and I'm sick to the back teeth of your usual ingratitude – we're all killing ourselves for you, as per, and all we get is insults.

Do you remember when I climbed the plum tree when I was six because you'd been foul to me, and I got stuck? When Dad wanted to call the Fire Brigade you just said, 'No, leave her, it'll teach her a lesson. She'll come down when she's cold and hungry. Either that or she'll *fall* out eventually'? That's pretty much the way I feel about you right now. The others, of course, being soppy, are trying to put a ladder up to you, which you keep kicking, but if Howard loses any more weight over this he'll be dead within a month.

Stop being so frigging selfish. Got to go – Sabrina's just puked down my neck.

Karen

The Vicarage,
Cynnington

Dear Trev,

Enc. some missives for Vera Smalls from her family and friends – thought I'd send them post haste, even though I'll be seeing you in a couple of days. We're going ahead with the beanfeast despite her disassociating herself from it, and just pray that she will see the light.

Fancy Pongo and Gerry still being together after all that falling out over the Transubstantiation! If only all Holy Wars could be so happily resolved!!

I'm encing a small notette from me to Mrs Smalls, too. I've heard the grub in there is pretty grot, so I've written it on (unsanctified) communion wafers. Tell her to pig the lot when she's read it.

Can't wait till Saturday – Sunday Mrs Wiggins is going to do us lamb en croute, so as soon as I get the silly old services out of the way, we can tuck in and get stinko like the good old days. Should more than make up for the load of old lentils we'll get at Sheepdipper's at the bash. For afters I've asked for Grand Marnier soufflé, her absolute speciality. Why the hell shouldn't we clergy enjoy ourselves? Tee hee, aren't I naughty? I've just been doing my parish rounds, and I've had a couple of sherries over the eight.

Peace and love,

Brucie Baby

1. The Vicarage,
Cynnington.
8th May
Dear Mrs Smalls –
PTO

I've written this on
communion wafers which –

please turn to next...

2. – means I can't get
much onto a page but –
PTO

at least you'll have
a square (or round, ha ha)
meal –
please turn to next ...

3. out of it. Your
friends and family
PTO

all love and miss you
and want more –
please turn to next ...

4. than anything to
help you come out
PTO

of prison. Being
insane is –
please turn to next ...

5. only a formality
to secure your
PTO

release. I am a man of
God and wouldn't –
    please turn to next . . .

6. deceive you. Please
trust us and help
PTO

us help you. Irene would
like nothing –
    please turn to next . . .

7. better than to prove
your innocence –
PTO

let her help you. I fear
for her
    please turn to next . . .

8. sanity if you don't
plead insane.
PTO

God bless and keep you,
Bruce.

c/o Sheepdipper's Shed
10th May

Dear Vera,

  I don't know what right you've got to get shirty with me, but we'll let that pass. If you're cross about your age in the paper, how do you think I felt about being called a buxom eighty-five? If you're cross about me saying you're insane, you must be mad. *I* am perfectly compos, but I wasn't too proud to be declared unsound of mind if that meant my liberty. Doing this literacy course is all very nice, but I don't think it'll help our case much – nor does my lady barrister, who I've hired to examine your briefs, and which she's been doing in detail since last Monday week. She's also trying to get Beefy an appeal, so has been going through her briefs as well. I can't begin to tell you what she's found there so far, but I do advise you to keep her sweet – she could turn at any moment.
  I am very happy to be 'out' despite the fact that I am working my fingers to the bone. Sabrina has nappy rash and colic, Karen's eczema has flared up again, Howard is down to nine stone two, Sidney's got enteritis and Antony's long awaited ingrowing toe-nail operation was not a success. But I'll tell you this – if they all had the bubonic plague I'd sooner be here than in that hell-hole of a prison ship. See sense and be insane. I'm sending you an avocado as I remember the warders think they're foreign muck, so might actually not steal it for themselves. Hope it's not too ripe by the time you get it. Write when you can – what am I saying? You're the leader of the literacy course. Write soon.

Best wishes,

Irene

15th May

Dear Bruce,

   Please see that all concerned get a copy of this letter. I appoint you executor of my property. Divide it as you think fit. As far as I'm concerned, you can give the lot to Oxfam.
   The communion wafers were a nice thought, though they do leave one rather dry. I missed the swig of Piat d'Or.

All the best,

Vera

P.S. Don't let Karen get her hands on the crystal – it would all be smashed in a fortnight.
P.P.S. Howard's always been fond of the photo of me that stands on the bedside table.

H.M. Prison Ship *Pride of Cleveland*

15th May

My Dear Friends,

After eating your letters I discussed them with my
therapist (a top Harley Street man, consigned to shipboard
duties after publicly announcing the Government was
barmy). He's against my declaring myself mad as, although I
am barking, it would cast aspersions on his abilities. He says
there's nothing wrong with me that fifteen years' Freudian
analysis won't put right, and as that's at least as long as I
shall be here, I might as well get the benefit. I must say I
thoroughly enjoy my sessions with him. It's not everyone
will listen while you ramble on about yourself. My
last-but-one cellmate begged to be put in solitary. I have
relived some momentous events from my childhood. There
was the time I stuffed Teddy down the lav and kicked my
dolls' house to pieces. I was reacting against being unloved
apparently, and all I can say is, I wish I'd made such a fuss
in my adult life. The times I wanted to strangle Gerald ...
now I'll never get the opportunity. When we aren't talking
about me, Arnon (my therapist) tells me about his problems
with his wife and family. These are considerably fewer of
course, with the Bay of Biscay between them. If neither of
us can think of anything to say we ask the 'I Ching', which is
rather obscure for my taste, or play Scrabble, which I love,
as I'm always on the look-out to enrich my vocabulary.
Arnon got hegemony yesterday. I tried that on my literacy
class and they got very excited.

I want you all to know that I attach no blame, no, not
even to Irene, though some of the things she has said about
me are certainly less than Christian. I'm sure she is getting
her come-uppance: she's much too old to be dealing with a

baby, and as for my erstwhile family, I wish her joy of them, Arnon says they are useless baggage. Beefy's been moved to another cell. She had taken to chewing the bars with her teeth, so desperate was she to free me. But I am not entirely alone. I have planted a little seed I found in my gruel in a crack in the wall. I have nothing to feed the poor thing with, but I crumbled a bit of communion wafer onto it and watered it liberally with my tears, so hopefully God will bless it.

Goodbye, my dears. I shall try to remember the good times we had. You may never see me again but I wish you joy on your side of the great water.

Forget about me.

Vera

P.S. I used the avocado as a face pack, it was too far gone for consumption.

Sheepdipper's Shed

20th May

Dearest darling Mums,

Why are you doing this to me? Have you forgotten how much I love you? Why are you doing it to yourself? Oh Mums, I've got alopecia – great scads of hair are falling out from every follicle on my body. I'm nearly bald. Mostly it happens at night, and in the morning the bed is like an animal's lair: the first morning it happened I woke up and thought that Antony was wearing a chest wig. He's being ever so sweet and supportive, but how long will it last? How can anyone love someone who looks like a boiled egg from behind? Mummy, please come and rescue me, I simply cannot bear it any longer.

The other dreadful thing is that Irene has disappeared. She said she was going underground for a while, so naturally I thought she'd gone to visit Blue John Mines, but when she didn't come back that night we all got really worried. Would she be silly enough to go pot-holing on her own? I do hope she's alright. It's ever such a strain here without her. Karen makes me and Antony babysit every night while she goes off to the pub, and she's always so *cross.*

Oh dear, dear. Two paragraphs already and I haven't said anything cheerful. Here goes. We had the Fork and Finger for your appeal and really, all things considered, it was quite a success. Jimmy Young couldn't make it in the end, as couldn't Selina Scott, Valerie Singleton, Gloria Hunniford, Terry Wogan, Esther Rantzen, Geoffrey Wainwright (MP for Shagthorne East [Con.]), Prince Charles or the Archbishop of Canterbury. However, Nigel Norris came from the *Gazette,* and because he's such a dear (he was one of the first friends I made when I moved to the area, and we were quite close for several months) he managed to rustle up Les Spatchcock to be our celebrity. You may remember that a couple of years ago Les qualified for the quarter finals of the British Snooker Contest at the Sheffield Crucible, which was televised nationwide, and for a couple of tense days the whole of Great Shagthorne held its breath. Les graciously consented to be photographed in all sorts of sporting poses for the *Gazette*, and spoke to us all on your behalf. I enclose the cutting, and hope you agree that he did a fine job to the best of his abilities. We had to guess at the Blue Cheese Dip – I sent some to you with Trevor, your prison chaplain, so you can judge for yourself the measure of our success. Personally I think there's at least one ingredient missing, but none of us could guess what it could be. Irene's roulade was its usual big hit, and I'm sending you a photograph of the celebration cake – I think Les was a bit squiffy by then!

Mums, I'm really pleased that you're having therapy and are sorting out your childhood – it took me three intensive, painful years to get over mine – but honestly there are much better facilities for that *out here*. There's a thriving alternative therapy centre right here in the village now, and I could book you a whole course of rebirthing, primal screaming, flotation, aromatherapy, reflexology and psychic healing for your birthday treat this year. Please think about it and discuss it with Arnon. Incidentally, Antony used to know an Arnon who was a therapist, but I don't imagine it was the same one. This one was struck off for the kind of unprofessional behaviour which is quite different from the sort you mentioned. Still, if it *is* the same one and you *are* thinking of indulging, do please wear a condom, Mummy – that is to say, get him to wear one rather, because things have changed since your day, and that brief moment of pleasure now can bring death and destruction later. But don't let me put you off.

I'm going to have to sign off now, reluctantly, as it's my turn to comb the sheep – honestly, you wouldn't believe how untidy they get – a farmer's work is never done!

Dearest sweetest darlingest Moo Ma (do you remember I used to call you that as a little boy? Aaaaah!) I've read and re-read all your letters over the last few weeks, and I simply cannot understand why you're being so intransigent. Is it just that you've become so institutionalised that you are afraid of life beyond your prison walls? If it is, we could help you through that. You could stay in your room for the first week – we could even *lock* you in if it made you feel more at home. Please think about it. And don't give up on the 'I Ching' – it changed my life back in '72, and I can never thank it enough.

Write soon. Or even better, come out soon.

All my love,
Your little
Howie
xxx
xx
x
!

THE TRAGIC STORY OF VERA SMALL

by *Shagthorne Gazette* Reporter

NIGEL NORRIS

LOCAL HERO Les Spatchcock (pictured above having a light-hearted moment with a french stick and an apple, 'Potting The Green') entertained a small but select crowd last Saturday at the Vera Small is Mad Appeal Fork and Finger Buffet.

Vera, mother of Howard Small of Sheepdipper's Shed — renowned throughout the length and breadth of Shale for his delicious organic sheep's yoghurt, available at attractive wholesale prices for bulk orders — claims that she was wrongly accused of being a drugs baron who preyed on the weak-willed and disillusioned in her native Little Potterton, and is currently awaiting trial on the high security prison ship, HMS *Pride of Cleveland*, at anchor off the east coast.

While Vera languishes in her cell, her family and friends are working tirelessly for her release. A regular churchgoer (I counted at least two dog-collars among the enthusiastic supporters) and a pensioner who served her country on the home front during the last war, Vera was a pillar of her local community, organising Bring and Buys, spearheading the campaign for compulsory poop-and-scoop for pet-owners on her village green and being an inspiration to the Friends of St Peter's flower arranging circle. Now, typically, she is refusing to appeal for bail or even to consider her defence, because she feels her work 'inside' among the prisoners is more important than her own personal survival. Anybody who watches 'Prisoner: Cell Block H' can imagine the appalling conditions under which she must be working, but nevertheless Vera Small is adamant that she will stay and do her duty, and try to succeed where government educational reforms have failed. So far her perseverance has succeeded — rumour has it that every prisoner on board HMS *Pride of Cleveland* can now write her own name.

(continued on page 2)

(continued from front page)

BUT VERA ISN'T STOPPING THERE

Speaking on her behalf, the prison chaplain Reverend Trevor Bull said, 'Vera won't rest until all her pupils can fill out a DHSS claim form without her help, and without copying from their neighbour. The prisoners are rising gallantly to the challenge, and when I last saw them two days ago, were busy sucking their pencils over "previous employment".'

If you would like to help the Vera Small is Mad Appeal, please send contributions c/o the *Gazette*. And if you're interested in the Vera Small Prisoners' Literacy Campaign and have any old books you no longer need, please send them direct to Vera Small, HMS *Pride of Cleveland*, The Wash.

(Now turn to page 23 to see Les Spatchcock in more serious mode at Clangham Leisure Centre Professional Snooker Exhibition.)

26th May

My dear Howard (It really is time you gave up your baby name, remember, you *are* nearly forty)

I'm very sorry about the hair. But I really don't see how I can be to blame. Arnon has taught me many things (I won't go into details just now, this letter may be censored) but the most important by far is to rush towards guilt less willingly. This is awkward for a person ready to admit to everything from the burning of a saucepan to the extermination of the Jews, but I find it easier in here where none of you can get at me. Frankly, dear, what you choose to do with your life is not my responsibility. Both of you children have unique gifts – if you count Karen's ability to shatter glass with her screams and cry long enough to qualify for the *Guinness Book of Records* – now, to quote Arnon's phrase, 'just get off your butts and use them!'

I wish I could describe to you the liberation I have felt in this prison cell. No mirrors to remind one of wrinkles and warts; no telephone to interrupt at an inconvenient moment; no dependants demanding love and protection; above all no friends, with their expectations of your behaviour and disappointment in it. Rest assured that wherever Irene is she will be in charge. If she is indeed 'underground', she will be bossing around the seven dwarves and teaching the nastier of the trolls they'd better mind their manners. Don't worry about her. She is a survivor. I must say, the prospect of seeing any of you again fills me with horror. Nor does the notion of living at Sheepshedders or whatever it's called enthrall me. Hessian is all very well in its place, which is not, in my opinion, on the walls. Wool next to my skin makes me itch, so there's no way I'm sleeping with a sheep on the bed. Then there's the toilet facilities – all that health food and only one loo! I

make do with a slop bucket here, but at least it is mine
exclusively. No, no, Howie, it wouldn't work. Of course, if
you were to consider the possibility of refurbishing the large
front room with manmade fibres and ensuite lavatory ...

Must rush now. It's play-reading class. We're on the
second act of *Les Miserables*, which has struck a chord with
many of the inmates.

Some of my love,

Vera

P.S. The mystery ingredient was your father's hair tonic.
I'm trying to remember what it was called so that you can
try some.

The Gables
Little Potterton

14th July

Dear Vera,

I don't suppose you'll be interested, since you have
apparently given up all concern for your erstwhile life
'outside', but I have moved into your old house for a while,
and thank heavens I did! Some young people had 'squatted'
in it (in more ways than one) and were charging admission
to Acid House parties. Of course word has got round locally
about your trouble with the police, and the teenagers think
you're marvellous for being an OAP drugs baron. The
tickets said 'Get off your face at Vera's place', whatever that
means. Anyway, I chased them out and have put the house
to rights as much as I can, although I'm afraid your crystal
has gone the way of all things, and your Aunty Gertie's
Victorian commode has had to be sent away to be destroyed.

I came here to get some peace away from Sheepdipper's
Shed, and to indulge in some quiet reflection. In that
respect I do miss prison life – being 'banged up' in solitary
can sometimes be a blessing. I sold my house when I came
out in order to pay our legal fees to the lady barrister and to
fund your appeal. There's still some money left, so don't
worry, I shan't be a drain on your resources, although I shall
have to be careful if it is to last me my days.

I'm sorry you've decided to give up your fight and spend
the rest of your allotted 'inside'. I had hoped that you and I
would spend a jolly retirement together, perhaps travelling
the world and doing everything that women of our
generation could never do when our husbands were alive.
Still, 'to each one his role' (Thought for the Day in today's
Daily Mirror), and who am I to keep you from your destiny?

There's a lot of work still to be done here, but I'm

tackling it little by little. The mint's done very well – it's taken over the entire garden – so I shall soon be bottling that like mad, as a sauce, to sell at the forthcoming Church Fete. Quite like old times, in a way, but somehow strangely different. The local community have welcomed me with open arms, and I have been invited to take over your position as Chairperson of the Little Potterton Poop and Scoop Campaign, which I have willingly undertaken. Of course, being a dog-owner lends a great deal of weight to the argument, and Sidney and I are busy setting a good example on the Village Green. There's also talk afoot of a new by-pass scheme which, if built, would come straight through your patio, thereby making your picture window more like a Space Invaders screen. While there is breath left in me I shall fight it, but let's hope it doesn't come to that – with my track record with bulldozers, we know where *that* would end!

I am enclosing a few pressed sprigs of lavender, mint and thyme to remind you of an English country garden – I hope they still smell by the time they reach you.

I had a postcard from Lesley the other day. Keith has left her for another woman, and she's wondering if I'd like to go out there to look after Cheryl Marie while she gets on with her new career in real estate. I was half-tempted for a second, but on reflection decided against. Once you've got used to the idea that you're dispensable, it's not an unattractive existence by any means. And after my recent experiences with Karen and Sabrina I intend to give a wide berth to spoilt children in future.

All for now as the Vicar's coming round in a minute in his capacity as Treasurer of the Poop and Scoop to discuss the inevitable fund-raising. Does it never end?! Glad to hear that you're well and happy and are at last feeling fulfilled,

Kindest regards,
Irene

Sheepdipper's Shed

22nd July

Dear Irene,

Snatching a few moments from washing nappies to put
pen to paper. Or rather, quill to recycled Papyrus – excuse
the bumps and blotches. Can't say I'm entirely happy with
the nappies, which have turned an unpleasant magenta ... is
it the ecology-conscious washing powder, or has Karen
been feeding beetroot to Sabrina? Frankly, nothing about
this place would surprise me. I have just cooked supper for
six adults (if you include Karen), a baby, twelve sheep, three
dogs, eleven cats, two goats and a donkey. Even Jesus would
have had trouble making a whole wheat loaf and a couple of
free range trout go round that lot.

They are so incompetent, I can quite see why you left.
Normally I enjoy restoring order to chaos, but this has got
me stumped. Today, Howard gave two sacks of butter beans
and a Celtic Craft poncho to a girl collecting for earthquake
victims and Antony put a nail through a pipe while trying to
build a sauna. Karen keeps to her room all day, thank
Heavens. She says she is 'proof-reading' but I heard the
distinct sound of snoring this afternoon. Hardly surprising,
as her nocturnal ramblings are becoming quite legendary.
She visits every pub in the village, then paddles on the pond
singing rude songs or absails from the belfry.

Apart from that, things go on as normal. Howard's been
fitted for an NHS wig. We were very supportive, but Karen
had to ruin it all by suggesting he could play Widow
Twankey. We have a visiting Swami who meditates on the
lawn and dyed my new underwear orange, and an
out-of-work actor chum of Howard's who is 'helping' in the
shop. Clearly he has been helping himself since the till has

been out three days running.

I've just realised you must be wondering what on earth I am doing here. The last time we communicated I was still 'inside'. Well ... whoops, there's been a terrible bang upstairs. Either Karen has fallen out of bed or Antony's blown up the central heating. Explanations soon, the availability of Papyrus permitting.

In haste,

Vera

P.S. Everyone's pleased to know you're alive and well, in their own way. Howard murmured, 'She was such a dear,' and Karen said, 'Who's Irene?'

P.P.S. What on earth do you mean, 'The mint has taken over'? I was *ruthless* with that patch for years. As soon as my back's turned, it runs amok. All I can say is, *be brutal*!

The Gables

28th July

My dear Vera,

Congratulations and felicitations! I can't get over the fact that you're back with us again – and in more ways than one, by the tone of your letter. I don't know which is more miraculous – your freedom or your friendliness. Thank goodness you're 'back to normal'. I tried to ring you, but I note that the Sheepdipper's phone has been cut off again. Howard is a hopeless businessman, I'm afraid to say. Last time he couldn't pay the bill because of cashflow problems he tried to barter with British Telecom with yoghurt. Imagine the administrative nightmares they would have had trying to distribute that to the share-holders!

Please do write post haste and tell me all about it. Better still, come over and see me *soon*. Do you want your house back, or are you going to stay with the children for a while? I can easily move out as soon as you say the word. Audrey Roscoe (I've re-established contact with her recently, and I'm pleased to say she's much pleasanter these days) keeps on at me to go and stay with her again, so I could go there. (I must tell you in full one day the laughs we had about Clive once we'd broken the ice between us – it seems as if his old 'problem' reared its head with her as well – or rather, didn't rear its head, if you get my meaning.) But I digress. Let me know what you want as soon as you know yourself. Sidney's barking – I've told him your good news and that I'm writing to you at the moment, so I imagine he's sending his 'best regards'!

I'm intrigued to know how your release came about, and am wondering if it was anything to do with my protest? I've been writing non-stop to the Home Secretary, and after getting nowhere for weeks, I told him that if he didn't let you out straight away, I would pull out my teeth one by one and send them to him daily. This I have been doing for the last fortnight, and was beginning to despair of a result being obtained before the full set gave out. Don't worry, your 'friend' is neither toothless nor gaga: I've been cracking them out of Clive's old dentures with a pair of pliers. I hung on to them at first through sentimentality, but I knew they'd come in useful one day.

The other thing I've been up to is trying to focus some psychic powers onto you (Bruce, of course, is up in arms about it – I sometimes don't know why the Christian Church is so paranoid and small-minded if they know they're in the right). I've spent a fortune on mystical literature and artefacts, and have read the Tarot, the Runes, the Tea-leaves and your hand (you'd left a nasty imprint on your mahogany wardrobe, which I've polished off now). And now you say that Karen's been doing it by reading the Proofs. What are they? I haven't come across them in my researches. You see, nobody is all bad. I'm sorry she's back drinking again, though. Antony gave her some special herbs to smoke instead, and they seemed to do the trick for a while, but I believe they are hard to come by and rather expensive. Really, you'd think that if the Department of Health was genuinely anxious about alcoholism that they'd give these things out on prescription, wouldn't you? I had a tiny go on them myself, and thoroughly enjoyed it, even though I'm not a smoker personally.

Anyway, all for now as I'm anxious not to miss the post, and Sidney is showing signs of wanting to set a shining example of poop and scoop hygiene on the Village Green. I am enclosing some sheets of your own personalised stationery so you can dispense with the papyrus. Honestly, the things we've written on lately! It's worse than the war with 'make do and mend'. It was lovely to hear from you –

such as welcome surprise – and I can't wait to see your old smiling face again. I shan't put 'with love', since it caused such a rumpus between us last time, but believe me, I do send you

My kindest, sincerest regards,

Irene

The Bluebell B & B
Lower Shagthorne
Derbs.

5th August

My Dear Irene,

At last I've had time to digest your letters properly.
Talking of digest, I'm relieved about the teeth. One turned
up in the *Cleveland*'s Sunday gruel but I assumed it was the
cook's – he and the sous chef had violent relations. As you'll
see, I've moved into a B & B in the village. Sheepdipper's
was getting me down, what with the cooking and chanting
and living life as a constant 'celebration'. And don't talk to
me about runes; Antony's up to his elbows in them!

Well, you'll be hopping with curiosity about my release.
It was all Arnon's doing. He explained to me that staying
'inside' was 'fulfilling my need to be needed' and that now
my literacy class had mastered *Janet and John* I could leave
them to themselves with the reading. I must say, keeping up
was becoming an effort. I mean, I love a good read but
Nietzsche *is* rather trying, especially without reading
glasses. Once I'd decided to make my bid for freedom,
Arnon took over. He said he'd give me some LSD (no, not
money, that's the mistake *I* made) and we'd leave the rest to
fortune. It was very dramatic. Apparently I shredded a sail
with my bare hands and splintered the deck with a hatchet,
then I shinned up the topmast, stripped and sang
'Jerusalem' and offered oral sex to the bo'sun. All I can
remember is seeing stars, but that was probably when they
knocked me out, as I came to in a straight-jacket. It was the
talk of the ship for days; there was no end of pipe-tapping.
Eventually the governor signed a release form putting me in
care of the community. It seems that if you are mad you are

safer on the outside; *every*one there is doolalley. Howard
and Antony came to fetch me and I saw my last glimpse of
HMS Cleveland from the back of their van – they'd
thoughtfully cut a couple of holes in the lentil sack I was
tied in.

It took me a while to recover. I kept getting 'flashes'
(rather like flushes, but brighter) but on my second day
Karen accused me of being lazy, so that got me up and
doing. From then till now I haven't sat down, except
cross-legged to do Yoga, and I am completely exhausted.

About the house – stay as long as you like, though I must
say, I *do* miss the garden. The shale at Shag is very
unrewarding. I often sat at my prison window gazing
through the bars at the restless waves and daydreaming of
Little Potterton's loamy pastures. Of course my lawn was
only twelve by eight but its verdant green was delightful.
How true those sentiments (Wordsworth's I think) about
being closer to God in a garden. Not, I'm afraid, that I
believe in God. There, I've said it. I'm sorry if it offends. I
know you've always been in close contact with the Divine
(or at least, with His earthly representatives) but I've come
to the conclusion that it's a gigantic con-trick to keep
women in their place. Ask yourself who it is who arranges
the flowers, irons the vestments, scrubs the flags, bakes the
cakes and yes, who sits in those uncomfortable pews while
some ridiculous twit drones on about duty and self
sacrifice? I confided my doubts to Rev. Trev (remember
him?) in the days after my shipboard frenzy. He said I
should use them in my testimony as further proof of
madness.

Your offer of a touring retirement in parts unknown is
certainly very attractive, but what, I wonder, would we fund
it with? Karen is trying to take over what remains of my
meagre resources (I've been paying the mortgage on
Sheepdipper's since before I went 'inside') on the grounds

that I'm officially insane, but so far I've resisted. Perhaps we should write a book about our exploits!

I'm so very tired I must lie down. Write soon with a few of your cheery words.

Your ever dear friend,

Vera

P.S. I can't recommend Audrey for an indefinite stay. She's a good soul, but she hasn't much of a sense of humour.
P.P.S. Of course, I am indispensable at Sheepdipper's. I run up there every day. Sabrina is teething and needs constant attention. When I pointed that out to Karen, she snarled that it was more than *she*'d got!

The Gables

10th August

Dear Vera,

Thank you for your letter. What an extraordinary story regarding your release! In fact, what an extraordinary turn our lives have taken altogether! It's almost as if we'd never lived before, what with the mundane round of bottling and jamming and bring and buys. And now we've both been in prison, both survived it stronger and wiser and with, I think, a stronger sense of life's adventure. The things we've seen and done! The words we've learnt! What *is* oral sex? You didn't bite him in the privates, did you?!

Be all that as it may, I can't help feeling rather depressed. We've lost so much. I've lost my home and you may lose yours. Another meeting of the Beat the Bypass group last night revealed that they are 99 per cent sure that they are going ahead, and will be compensating owners to a ridiculously low level, based on the poor current house prices. After all our pressuring, the only change they've made to their plans is to shift it over a few feet so that it will now come straight through your lounge instead of running outside it. I mean, what kind of a bypass is that?! I don't think the group is going to fight it any more. To be honest, they've got everything to gain by not doing. Yours and Mabel Thrush's old house are the only ones to be affected, and the rest of them will enjoy the benefits of no longer having juggernauts getting stuck on the bend at the Jolly Jackdaw. The new people at Mabel's were going to leave anyway due to a posting abroad (lucky them), and they're pretty relieved, what with the property market, that they'll get any money at all.

So what to do? Where to go to live out our days? And what on? Now that I know you're safe and well, I've been concentrating my psychic powers on drawing good luck and money to us both. I don't know if it's had any effect your end, but so far nothing has happened here. I tend to agree with you about God and the church – it *is* all a con trick to keep us in our place. But I feel very strongly that there *must* be something else, some reason for living, some rhythm to life, some force of good (and equally of evil), some Otherness or Isness linking us all to the whole, or *some*thing. Damn it – someone at the door, just when I'd got into my flow. Hang on.

Well! I don't know what to say! You'll never guess what's happened now. My dear – my prayers are answered! I can't believe it can be true! You remember the demo at Grossthorpe Links which led to my arrest – how could you forget! As always, we desperately needed funds at the time, so Arthur Snushall organised a raffle, and I showed willing by buying two books. After all this time, the blithering thing has been drawn, and I've won – First Prize! And you'll never guess what it is – a Dormobile camping van, fully fitted and equipped, donated by Ted and Marie Bellman after they splashed out on their Winnebago. It's a *home*, Vera, on *wheels*! What adventures we could have! Are you game? DO say yes! Let's take off and see the world – I've always wanted to, but never got past Marbella.

Vera, this proves my point – there *is* a purpose to prayer and positive thinking, and magic *does* exist. Even my tea-leaves indicated something of this nature this morning, but I was too down in the mouth to take any notice. Vera, I dare you to come with me and see the world – what have we got to lose? Write back sooner than soon, and heigh ho Silver, away!

Your buccaneering friend,

Irene

P.S. And what would Arnon say about your P.P.S.? Break the mould! Be irresponsible and dispensable before you die!

The Bluebell B & B

14th August

My Dear Irene,

My first response to your letter was a whoop of joy. Only the Bluebell's pet parrot responded, the rest of the residents being too deaf, or perhaps dead, to notice. How wonderful to have nothing, except for Ted and Marie's Dormobile of course, and how timely your news. Yesterday I heard that my bank manager has made some terrible errors with standing orders (victim of an illness known as 'Business Lunch syndrome'). As a result I have defaulted on all mortgage and life insurance payments and the building society are about to repossess. Let them. See how they enjoy living in the fast lane. Literally. I'll cash in what's left of the life insurance – I was only hanging on to it to pay for my funeral – and Up, Up and Away! I can't wait to be tucked up in those dear little bunk beds. I'm so over the moon (would the moon be going *too* far d'you think?) I'm going to make myself a cup of hotel-bedroom instant coffee to celebrate!

Later.
There's only one thing. I won't be doing all the driving. Now you've passed your test there's no excuse, and I can't abide a back-seat driver. I'll never forget you punching me in the ear as you 'instructed' me with hand gestures to 'go round the bend' on the Horseshoe Pass. We were lucky to escape with minor injuries. No. Irene, it's in the front and behind the wheel, or we'll be going nowhere.

Later.
By the by, how big *is* this Dormobile? Space is so important in relationships, Arnon taught me that. I mean, I

wouldn't call you *territorial,* exactly, but you did put all my things in the corner when I stayed and cover them with a dust-sheet. You were also particular on soiled undies, I recall. You gave me a plastic carrier bag so they wouldn't sully the bedroom. Then there are other ... more 'personal' ... functions. A home on wheels is just the place to discover the worst about toilet training. As for possessive! I thought you were going to call the police the day I went out with your brolly. How will you be with the foreign food? You can't abide a Coquille St Jacques and the natives are devils for garlic. Come to that, how will you be with the natives? Oh dear, oh dear, I *am* sounding churlish and after your lovely letter ... But I can't help feeling that we've had our ups and downs and that was when we were living apart. How will we be *together?*

Still later.

Rushed up to Sheepdipper's with a matinée jacket I've been crocheting in the evenings. They were all in a terrible state about the money. Howard was weeping into a soya bean casserole and Karen had hit the vodka bottle. She wasn't a bit grateful for the jacket and said what was I trying to do, make ethnic history by getting Sabrina to win the Miss Pears competition? I didn't say anything. Later when she told me it was time for Sabrina's bath I pointed out that it was her turn, Sabrina was *her* baby. She gave me a very peculiar look and snapped she was glad I'd remembered. I think Antony was sorry for me. He gave me a set of runes so I'm throwing them madly.

Next morning.

The runes said journey so I've settled my bill. Popped into the library for some Linguafone records – I know you're a stickler for pronunciation. I got French, Italian, German, Spanish, Cameroons, Hindu and Swahili. N.B.

Must remember to get an international driving licence. You too.

Later.
   Last visit to Sheepdipper's to say goodbye. Howard's very excited. He's found a financial backer – some local chap who'd been dabbling in stripped pine, then his partner went off with another chap and now he wants something substantial. The soya bean casserole should be just the ticket. Showed Karen how to care for the seeds I've sown and tended. I'm wasting my time, they'll be dead in a week. She doesn't know a radish from a nettle. I'm popping down to Buxton for a couple of days to buy some suitable clothing – there's nothing more adventurous than a duvet coat in Shagthorne.

> The Bull & Pestle
> Dyke Lane
> Buxton

   I've spent up. A lurex sarong, striped beach outfit, emerald taffeta ballgown, cerise cocktail number, two dozen espadrilles and a gorgeous two-piece bathing suit for you in primrose and vermilion. Drop me a note at the above. All being well I leave Friday.

Next morning.
   Woke in tears with a terrible sense of loss. Oh Irene, we will be alright, won't we?

The Gables

19th August

Dear Vera,

My first response to *your* letter was, 'Alright then, forget it'. Talk about looking a gift horse in the mouth and recommending orthodontistry! Talk about ungrateful, ungracious and just plain bloody rude! Talk about limiting somebody's growth potential by reminding them that they are the nastiest, most unreasonable person you know, and implying that any change for the better is impossible. Really, it sometimes seems to me that you regard yourself as the perfect centre of a disappointingly imperfect universe. Haven't you learnt *anything* at *all* through all your psychotherapy? Or does it only apply to you? Oh yes, it's all very well for *you* to carp and cavil – we're all in the wrong, you're the only one in the right. Have you ever stopped to wonder why both your children turned out to be total incompetents?

But my second response was, 'Rise above it Irene, she's probably over-tired'. Certainly, I can think of no other reason that you'd spend all your petrol money on ball gowns and lurex sarongs. And why buy me a bikini? Do you think I can't look after my *own* beachwear? Personally I am travelling light, and I can tell you now that the Dormobile is *small,* so unless your emerald taffeta folds down to the size of a pacamac, forget it.

My third response – and you'll see I'm getting it more in perspective and feeling less angry all the time – is that it is only right and proper for you to express your fears, as it is only right and proper for me to express mine. Yes, you've hit the nail on the head, change is very frightening. But what's the alternative? What use has fear been to us all our lives? It

144

kept me unhappily married to a man who despised me, who told me I was a fool, and who couldn't keep his hands off our dinner guests. I'm damned if I'm going to make the same mistake twice, particularly at this late stage in my journey through life. 'Onwards, ever onwards' is *my* battlecry for the rest of my allotted, but don't let me stop you from staying rooted in the mire of your own misery until death do you part, I'm sure.

My fourth response – and now I'm getting calmer and more constructive all the time, as I think you'll agree – is to reassure you that we'll work it out if we both keep our senses of humour and try to live and let live. If, for instance, it proves to be that I can't stand being cooped up in a confined space with your dreadful, earth-shattering snoring, I shall try to maintain the attitude that you're not doing it for the sole purpose of driving me round the bend, to borrow your phrase. And talking of which, I intend to do *most* of the driving, thank you very much, particularly as it seems that I shall be buying the petrol.

But just in case we temporarily lose our sense of humour and our easy-going attitudes, perhaps we should make a rule. Like counting to ten before we speak again. Or saying 'Sollocks' like Amanda and Elyot in *Private Lives*. (I played Amanda to Cyril Organ's Elyot in 1958, and even Clive had to admit that my performance was hysterical.) Or, and perhaps this might be best of all and most apposite for us, maybe we should only communicate in writing if we're having a set-to, thereby giving a chance for tempers to cool and reason to take over. Think about it. The world is very large, as Elyot told Amanda, and it's going to take us a very long time to get round it, Vera, so we're going to have to pack a great deal of patience and humour. But then, what else has a life with Clive fitted me for, I ask myself?

So, if you feel up to the challenge, I shall pick you up at the Bull and Pestle at 10.00 a.m. on Friday, and we'll motor straight down to Dover, cross on the ferry, and be in France by the time the sun is over the yardarm. Here's to it! The next time we communicate in writing will be because one *or other* of us is being selfish and unreasonable, I imagine, so I'll take this opportunity of reminding you (in writing, so you don't forget) that I am very fond of you, despite all your foibles, and I wish you only happiness, contentment, and great adventures!

Sincerest and heartfelt regards,

Irene x

(An autoroute outside Calais)

Irene!

When I screamed Right! Right!
I was not agreeing that the driver of
the approaching truck was a "blithevin'
froggie cretin". I, like him, was in fear
for my life, they <u>drive</u> on the
right in this country!

P.S. I counted to ten before I wrote
    this, but at this rate it needs
    to be forty.

V.

TURN BACK THE CLOCK

Joyce Grenfell

TURN BACK THE CLOCK is the definitive collection of the much-loved Joyce Grenfell's best sketches and songs. Of the many treasures included within are the unforgettable *The Women's Institute Lecturer*, the marvellous *Nursery School Sketches* and the impeccably observed *Opera Interval*.

'Her characterisations are brilliant: with just a few words she's able to give you a deep and accurate picture of the person she "is" at that moment'
The Lady

'She writes in an easy conversational manner, so that you can almost hear her telling it to you'
The Financial Times

'If Joyce Grenfell's performances make you laugh, her monologues are just as funny to read . . . and will stand a lot of re-reading'
Church Times

FUTURA PUBLICATIONS
NON-FICTION/HUMOUR
0 7088 4903 2

GEORGE – DON'T DO THAT

Joyce Grenfell

Now, children, I want you all to say 'Good morning' to Mrs Hingle. Good morning, Mrs Hingle.

No, Sidney, not good-bye. Mrs Hingle has only just come. You don't want her to go away yet?

No, she hasn't got a funny hat on, that's her hair.

So sorry, Mrs Hingle. Sometimes we ARE just a trifle outspoken. We try to encourage honesty, only sometimes it doesn't always . . .

And this is my friend Caroline, and Caroline is painting such a lovely red picture, aren't you, Caroline? I wonder what it is? Perhaps it's a lovely sunset, is it? Or a big red orange?

It's a picture of Mummy! For a moment I thought it was a big red orange, but now you tell me, I can see it is a picture of Mummy.

Aren't you going to give her any nose?

No nose.

It's so interesting the way they see things . . .

FUTURA PUBLICATIONS
NON-FICTION/HUMOUR
0 7088 4774 9

JOYCE GRENFELL
REQUESTS THE PLEASURE

Joyce Grenfell

A legendary entertainer, Joyce Grenfell won the love of millions through her films, her stage and television performances, and her writing. This first volume of her autobiography takes the story from her childhood through the war, to the moment in 1945 when her own show, *Joyce Grenfell Requests the Pleasure*, opened in London.

'*Joyce Grenfell Requests the Pleasure* does for a girlhood in the twenties what books like Gwen Raverat's "Period Piece" or Joan Evans's "Prelude and Fugue" did for an earlier generation. Like those classics of childhood recollection, it is vivid, evocative, bathed in warm clear light and packed with the kind of curious lore one could pick up nowhere else'
Observer

'Read, re-read, laugh and cry over this unique book, but don't lend it to anyone, because if you do you'll never see it again'
Books and Bookmen

'Innumerable merry moments . . . It is to her own contented life that *Joyce Grenfell Requests the Pleasure* of a visit from you and me. Accept the invitation *at once*'
Sunday Telegraph

'Gripping . . . Joyce Grenfell's brilliant book is a success in the same sense and for the same reasons as are her performances'
The Times

FUTURA PUBLICATIONS
NON-FICTION/AUTOBIOGRAPHY
0 7088 4762 5

LIFE'S A BITCH ... AND THEN YOU DIET

Serena Gray

'A woman can never be too thin'
Nancy Reagan

'Most women are a diet just waiting to happen'
Sadie Gray

WHAT'S WRONG WITH YOUR BODY?

It is your hips? Your thighs? The size of your bum? Have you ever been on a diet? Only one? For how long have you been on a diet? A week? A month? More than five years?

If you're not on a diet now, will you be on one tomorrow? Next week? Right after you finish those chocolate biscuits?

Let's face it. Most of us worry about our weight most of the time. Rare is the woman who has never been on a diet. Rare the woman who isn't about to start a diet. Rarer still the woman who can say with a smile that she thinks her body is perfect as it is.

If you are one of the millions of women who wishes she were thinner, that her thighs were harder, that pizza didn't go straight to her hips, or that someone would invent the two-calorie chocolate gateau, then this is the book you've been waiting for.

FUTURA PUBLICATIONS
NON-FICTION/HUMOUR
0 7088 4853 2

BEACHED ON THE SHORES OF LOVE

Serena Gray

'A single woman over thirty-five has more chance of
being shot by a terrorist than of finding a man'
Newsweek

You are an intelligent, attractive, sophisticated and
independent woman. You have a good job, a terrific flat, a
fantastic record collection, hundreds of interesting,
exciting friends, great legs, holidays in the Himalayas and
a leather mini-skirt. You don't need men. You can open
your own jars, fix your own car, and leave your own sock
on the floor. You, survivor of more than one relationship
that has put both your stamina and your sense of humour
to the test, can do very nicely on your own, thank you
very much. Let others join dating clubs and singles
groups. And yet, every now and then, you sometimes hear
yourself say things like, 'I really hate champagne dinners
for one.' Still find yourself wondering if the man who
signs himself Lonely in Luton in the personals might be
half as good as he sounds. Still secretly root for
Cinderella. Still think that, someday, your prince is going
to come.

FUTURA PUBLICATIONS
NON-FICTION/HUMOUR
0 7088 4322 0

HOT BREATH

Sarah Harrison

'Funnier than Tom Sharpe'
Daily Mirror

Thirty-five, fit and solvent with children at school and the
sweet scent of freedom in my nostrils, I was ripe
for it . . .

What has transformed Harriet Blair, contented wife and
mother and bestselling author of torrid hot historicals into
a rampant vamp?

Could it be the arrival in sleepy Basset Parva of
Constantine Ghikas, blond Greek god and latest addition
to the local medical practice?

With husband George safely marooned in the Middle
East, Harriet feels the Fates have conspired to throw a
real-life romantic hero in her path. But her carefully-
staged seduction scenes are thwarted by the unwitting
sabotage of family and friends. Not to mention the
demands of her publishers, panting for the new
masterpiece . . .

Hell-bent on indulging her dishonourable intentions,
Harriet lurches from crisis to hilarious crisis, delighting
and entertaining everyone who has ever cast a greedy eye
over forbidden fruit . . .

FUTURA PUBLICATIONS
FICTION
0 7088 2954 6

All Futura Books are available at your bookshop or newsagent, or can be ordered from the following address:

Futura Books,
Cash Sales Department,
P.O. Box 11,
Falmouth,
Cornwall TR10 9EN.

Alternatively you may fax your order to the above address. Fax No. 0326 76423.

Payments can be made as follows: Cheque, postal order (payable to Macdonald & Co (Publishers) Ltd) or by credit cards, Visa/Access. Do not send cash or currency. UK customers: please send a cheque or postal order (no currency) and allow 80p for postage and packing for the first book plus 20p for each additional book up to a maximum charge of £2.00.

B.F.P.O. customers please allow 80p for the first book plus 20p for each additional book.

Overseas customers including Ireland, please allow £1.50 for postage and packing for the first book, £1.00 for the second book, and 30p for each additional book.

NAME (Block Letters) ....

ADDRESS ....

....

☐ I enclose my remittance for _____

☐ I wish to pay by Access/Visa Card

Number ⬚⬚⬚⬚⬚⬚⬚⬚⬚⬚⬚⬚⬚⬚⬚⬚⬚⬚⬚

Card Expiry Date ⬚⬚⬚⬚